JACK MURPHY

Abe and Me

818

Illustrated by
Chuck Beebe

Joyce Press, Inc.
San Diego, California
1977

Most of the material in this book orginally appeared in The San Diego Union and various newspapers subscribing to Copley News Service. Special thanks is given for permission to reprint it.

Introduction

When the body that lived at your single will, with its whimper of welcome, is stilled (how still!).
When the spirit that answered your every mood is gone — wherever it goes — for good, you will discover how much you care,
and will give your heart to a dog to tear.

Rudyard Kipling wrote that, and it's pretty good. But it isn't any better than Jack Murphy and the thousands of words he wrote about his dear friend who just, incidentally, happened to be a dog.

Being in the same sort of dodge as Jack, that of writing a daily column, I have always envied him and his pieces of Abe of Spoon River. Jack and Abe could go out in the fields or woods and have a glorious, close day, and then Jack could come into his office, light up his ever-present pipe, and enjoy the day all over again at his typewriter.

"Abe and Me" is a man's, woman's and child's book. It is a love story of great beauty.

John Sinor

Red Smith Says...

In February of 1977, a car struck Abe of Spoon River and wiped out a part of Jack Murphy's life. Abe was a Labrador Retriever who was Jack Murphy's friend and hunting companion for 13 years. He was black, black as half past midnight except for a fringe of white that age brought to his chin toward the end. He must have been invisible that last evening on a dark road in Poway, California.

A day or so after Abe's death, Jack sat in his office at The San Diego Union, where he is sports editor, looking at something like 200 letters of condolence, mostly from readers he had never met. Over and over they repeated the same question: "Can't we have a book about Abe?"

"A book ought to have some excuse for being written," Joe H. Palmer wrote in the foreword of a book he never finished. "Often this is left to the reader to discover, and all too frequently it is hidden too cleverly for him."

The excuse for this book, if it needs one, is popular demand. Though readers of The Union who felt a sense of personal loss when Abe died did not know it, the book was already in preparation when they wrote. Over the years, many other readers had made the same request.

It may be that Abe was known to more people more intimately than any other dog, and that more strangers felt kinship with him. (Lassie doesn't count because there have been so many of her in movies and on television, all males.) Jack Murphy loves to hunt, and it was a poor day when he and Abe came home from the field without material for another warm column. Though they pretended to each other that they were hunting birds, Jack was always out hunting columns.

Jack had hunted and fished the Western United States from Baja California to Montana through all the 25 years since quitting Oklahoma, where he had fallen in love with the outdoors as a boy. He is no great menace to fish, and in some respects he is a peculiar sort of hunter. No matter how often he goes into the field and no matter how tempting the target, he refuses to squeeze the trigger early in the deer season because if he shot a deer he couldn't go deer hunting again. He will take his chances with quail, ducks and doves but he will not shoot a goose because honkers mate for life. For a devotee of blood sports, he is perhaps, deficient in bloodthirst.

Abe was bred to hunt. He enjoyed it above all else. Yet if he regarded his companion's peculiarities as flaws, he was too much the gentleman to indicate it. Between them there was mutual respect, understanding and affection. People are sometimes frustrated by a breakdown of communications, but never a man and his dog.

The columns reproduced here reveal Jack Murphy as the bright, particular star of Southern California journalism. At his best, two qualities stand out — a talent for putting the reader comfortably there on the scene, and the restraint that is born of good taste. He can write from the deep heart's core, unafraid of sentiment but never mawkish.

"One definition of a gentleman," Jack wrote, "is a man who can disagree without being disagreeable. It also serves to describe my friend Abe of Spoon River, a most elderly Labrador Retriever who disputes the judgment of his personal physician but does it with style and diplomacy."

That is from a column about Abe's last hunting season. Because he was old and deaf and his heart was unreliable, the veterinarian had advised against further hunting but Abe and Jack overruled the doctor. The column served notice to all those strangers who were Abe's friends that their friend wouldn't be around much longer.

Chapter 1

HOW IT BEGAN

A writer I admire was shopping a manuscript around to various publishers and he chuckled when one returned it with the comment: "These stories have trees in them."

The reader also will find trees in this collection of pieces which represent a segment of my work in The San Diego Union over the past dozen years. The central character is a Labrador Retriever who held me on a short leash from the moment I became his guardian in 1964 until his death on February 7, 1977.

I began writing about Abe of Spoon River — the name my son and I chose for him — because the dog pleased me greatly and I wanted to share my joy.

In other words, I decided to indulge myself. I sought an occasional escape from the structured world of sports, especially professional sports, where many cranky voices are heard. In theory, the sports section of a newspaper is a place to browse for entertainment, a refuge from the grim events of the day. But too often it is filled with the arguments of lawyers and agents; it seldom has the grace note of laughter.

Since boyhood, I have been excited by nature. I've had a kinship with most creatures, great and small. I captured a young squirrel who became so trusting he would feed from my hand and sleep on my shoulder. To the dismay of my saintly mother, I adopted a Great Horned Owl who required repair for a broken wing. The family garage became a roost for a flock of pigeons. Pigeons leave messes.

The great American Painter, Andrew Wyeth, has expressed something of what I feel about nature: "I can think of nothing more exciting than just sitting in a cornfield on a windy day and listening to the dry rustle. And when I walk through the rows of blowing corn, I am reminded of the way a king must have felt walking down the long line of knights on horseback with banners blowing."

My recreation, my fun, is hunting and fishing. Some readers find conflict in a man who says he reveres nature, yet kills birds and fish with gun and rod. Yet all the creatures of nature are hunters. Man is merely the most intelligent predator.

I learned about hunting partridges from naturalist Aldo Leopold in his treasure of philosophical musings, "A Sand County Almanac." Leopold counseled that one should "wander quite aimlessly, from one red lantern to another. This likely will take you where the birds are. The lanterns are blackberry leaves, red in the October sun. Red lanterns have lighted my way on many a pheasant hunt..."

My guide was Abe of Spoon River. Sometimes he led me to blackberry bushes busy with quail; more often he flushed them from chaparral and cactus. It is the custom of our family that everybody works and contributes, everybody but our decorative tomcat, Clovis.

Abe earned his keep, he fetched me birds and readers.

Long ago I made the happy discovery that a dog is truly a man's best friend, especially if the man is a writer. Abe's popularity delighted me, he became part of my identity. His admirers sent Christmas and birthday greetings; they worried when he was ill or infirm; they mourned when he died after being struck by a car.

Readers related to Abe because they recognized his endearing qualities in Shep and Duke and Lassie, their canine friends. I suspect they reasoned that a fellow lucky enough to keep company with Abe couldn't be all bad.

These pieces follow Abe from cradle to grave. They also deal with a few of my hunting and fishing campanions — notably Bob Jordan, a gentle game warden who tutored me about Labrador Retrievers and gave me a fascinating course in nature appreciation; Bill Tellam, cattleman, a bird hunter and cowboy Charles Russell would have loved to paint; and Red Smith, a witty, erudite fly caster who modestly describes himself as a Hall of Fame fish killer.

Forty years ago Smith brought a standard of literacy to sports writing which gives meaning to the bromide that some of the best writing in newspapers appears on the sports pages. True — if the writer is Red Smith.

While these pieces were being written and published, my son, John Patrick, grew to manhood; my daughter, Robin, got married and began raising children; my wife achieved her ambition to make a home in a semi-rural area and stick her green thumb into the soil; we acquired several cats who entertained us in their separate ways, and some of the people mentioned have died or divorced.

Jay Odell, now 88, who sent Abe to me at bargain rates, has lost his beloved wife, the Duchess, after 62 years of marriage.

Heathcliff, the black tom who smelled like a dog, succumbed to a mysterious disease.

Isaac, Son of Abraham, was no great success as a Labrador Retriever. Ike was pretty, he was lovable, but he avoided work. He wouldn't fetch fallen birds. We asked waivers on Ike.

Our two alley cats, Clovis and Clotilde, have survived in a dangerous environment. Coyotes have feasted on much of the cat population in our neighborhood; Clovis lost the tip of his tail and some of his dignity. Clotilde, shaggy and spirited female, is intact.

The cats get their names from history, and from a young historian. My son names the cats. Clovis was a French king of the fourth century who married a devoutly religious princess, Clotilde. Her ambition was to convert him to Christianity but Clovis was a hard sell. He died a pagan.

This book reflects the interests, the habits, the enthusiasms, of the writer. Red Smith applauds me as a conservationist among fishermen (I seldom have a fish to clean) and a fearless hunter who has never taken a backward step from a quail or pheasant, no matter how dangerous the circumstances.

Yet I loosely fit Smith's description of a fisherman. The three motivations of an angler, he reasons, are self-preservation, the reproductive urge, and a compulsion to try the other side of the lake, river or planet.

It is the compulsion to try the other side of the mountain that led us to Montana where we became landholders. There we have 70 acres of trees and pasture, a brook where trout bathe and eat, and sweet solitude.

I go there to fish and loaf, but it would be a fine place to write. One rule of writing says that a man can wander as far as he wants from the typewriter so long as he doesn't leave the property. I could work on a long leash in Montana.

Our Montana acreage is an expression of my wife's pioneering spirit. She's a cheerful, woodsy woman with a passion for the earth; she bought the ranch in the winter of 1972 while I was attending the Sapporo Olympics.

When Patricia first visited the log house on Truman Creek she had to make her way on snowshoes. A winter storm had left drifts which hid the barbed wire fences. But she could visualize it in spring; she swiftly signed the documents of possession.

As it happened, my birthday fell during the Winter Games on Hokkaido and I decided to treat myself to a chat with Patricia, and never mind the cost.

"Guess what," she greeted me from the other side of the world, "you're now a rancher in Montana."

We have glad times there in summer and I am reminded of a passage from "Three Men In A Boat" by Jerome K. Jerome: "Let your boat of life be light, packed with only what you need — a homely home and simple pleasures, a cat, a dog, a pipe or two, enough to eat and enough to wear and a little more than enough to drink; for thirst is a dangerous thing."

Chapter 2

THE THRILL OF HUNTING

Recollect that the Almighty, who gave the dog to be the companion of our pleasures and our toils, hath invested him with a nature noble and incapable of deceit.
Sir Walter Scott

I suppose you would say my friend Jay Odell is a senior citizen because he is in his 81st year, but he certainly isn't an old man.

It's the dogs, the Labrador Retrievers, that keep him young.

The ladies find his charm irresistable even though he sometimes toots on a dog whistle to attract attention when he feels ignored during a bridge party.

"If you were my husband, I wouldn't trust you out of sight," my wife once told him. Jay preened at that. He thinks my wife is wonderful and he has a high regard for her judgment.

It was Abe of Spoon River who brought Jay into our lives, or vice versa. Abe came to us from Odell's Consort Kennels, a farm near Crystal Lake, Ill. We consider him a remarkable dog because he fetches both birds and friends.

I first became aware of Odell when he wrote from Crystal Lake, offering me an opportunity to buy Abe (then unnamed) for the absurdly low price of $300. I sent him a courteous reply, explaining that I didn't have $300 to spend on a dog.

Soon another letter arrived, reducing the price to $200. Again, I declined with thanks.

Then one morning the phone rang and I heard my secretary saying a Mr. Odell was calling from Illinois. It was our first conversation, and I quickly learned that Jay isn't easily discouraged.

"Now listen," he said, "I want you to have this dog."

"That's very nice of you, Mr. Odell, but..."

He cut me off. "But nothing," he roared, "you love dogs, don't you?"

"Sure."

"Well, I know you can dig up $100 and pay for his transportation. I'm putting him on a flight at O'Hare Field tomorrow morning. He's yours if you pay the air freight; send me the $100 when it's convenient.

That seemed a generous proposition, and I was pleased to accept. I put the first of four $25 payments in the mail and went to Lindbergh Field to meet Abe.

He was then a pup of four months, slender and shiny, and we didn't require a formal introduction. When I opened the door to the kennel, the little fellow climbed into my arms and pushed his moist nose against my face.

It must have been a year later, long after I had started hunting with Abe and writing an occasional column about him, when I finally met Jay Odell. But we knew each other through the mail and on the telephone and already he was referring to me as his "California Pal".

Jay had sent me elaborate instructions about the care and feeding of Labradors. Then came James Lamb Free's helpful book on training Labradors and a four-page, single-spaced letter from Odell's trainer, Eddie Carey.

"Never be harsh with him," cautioned the trainer.

"Labradors are as sensitive as people, and they're a lot more noble than some people. All they really ask is a chance to please their master."

Splendid advice, that. And easy to follow. We got to know each other so well, Abe and I, we can communicate without language. And that's the main difference between Abe and Jay. Jay has a keen appreciation of the spoken work. He's the bird shooting version of Casey Stengel. He doesn't make statements, he tells stories.

The other day I asked him if he had ever visited Palomar Mountain and the answer took something like 30 minutes; that's when I learned how he happened to buy the pink house in La Jolla. But mostly he talks about Labradors, talks about them endlessly and entertainingly, and it's not a good idea to introduce an alien subject.

In one of the few concessions he makes to his years, Jay wears a hearing aid for a faulty ear and he hears best when the topic concerns dogs. Occasionally his sweet spouse, Ruth, the one he married 50 years ago, tries to divert him. Usually the effort is wasted.

"Jay," Ruth will ask, "why is it you can hear Jack when you can't hear me?"

Jay Odell is a man worth indulging. He addresses his wife as the Duchess and he adores her.

"My friend," he will say, "I can only wish you the happiness we've known for 59 years." Then pondering his good luck he adds, "And I'm not an easy man to live with either."

He's a big handsome guy with a strong face, broad shouldered and sturdy, and he has the vitality of a young man. Every night he has 10 hours of dreamless sleep, the bad ear shutting out the sounds of the street, and he looks fresher than men half his age on those early mornings when he arises to go wing shooting.

Sometimes he goes along just to watch the dogs work and, as he tells it, to get away from the domestic chores Ruth assigns him. A lovable friend, this man. Nothing pleases him more than hard work and lately he's been painting the pink house in La Jolla, the one he bought to complement the place in Florida and the farm in Illinois.

He is wealthy, I assume, and he says he is retired. But he sure isn't idle. Not with 30 dogs on the Bull Valley Farm, and Labs competing in the state field trial events to earn points for the national championship, and the bird hunting season approaching in Illinois.

He bought the farm, a beautiful place, for the dogs. And for a better reason. "The Labs make me feel young," he says. "I sometimes wish I were 65 again. There are lots of things I'd like to do."

First, though, he'll have to finish painting the house and get down off that ladder.

YUMA — We knew it would be awkward, leaving Duke behind, and I fear we didn't handle the situation with much tact. He watched with sad, accusing eyes as we stored the hunting gear. He had an air of bewilderment as we drove away with an attitude of feigned nonchalance.

It would have been kinder, perhaps if his attention had been diverted by breakfast or some form of deception. We even considered covering his eyes with a blindfold.

But Duke saw it all. Not only the hunters with their guns and the apparel they wear on such occasions, but the young Labrador Retriever who was sitting in the place he regarded as his own.

Thus, the torch passed from generation to generation. This was to be my first hunting experience with the new boy on the block - a shiny, frisky pup I had named Abe of Spoon River. It was a bittersweet moment.

I was excited about Abe, I sensed he had much promise, I anticipated many pleasurable hours in his company. But this was a melancholy occasion because Duke is a special friend, my first Labrador friend.

It was through Duke I learned to appreciate the joy of associating with Labrador Retrievers. I have no quarrel with people who prefer other breeds, but I am openly partisan to Labradors, and Duke is responsible for my bias.

He has been the owner of a mutual friend, Bob Jordan, for most of his 11 years and he also has claim on my affections. The three of us have shared many happy days, never quarreling, never complaining, and we rejoiced in our friendship.

But time has done its work on Duke. The old chap is becoming gimpy, he tires easily, he gets around with some difficulty. Now we are going to Arizona for dove shooting, and it was feared Duke might be harmed by the fierce heat of September in the desert.

Reluctantly, Jordan scrubbed Duke from the roster for this trip. It was a wrenching experience. We remembered so well when Duke had such vitality we envied him; he seemed invulnerable.

We had been providing birds for Duke to retrieve for nearly a decade, we didn't believe the day would arrive when we'd be going off without him. I was confident he'd always be waiting by the car, eyes brimming with excitement, his busy tail giving expressions to his elation.

Alas, this was a form of self-deception. Duke had become a pensioner, and a rookie had been summoned to take his place in the lineup.

I thought young Abe was a likely prospect because he had apprenticed at Duke's side. The old dog and the pup were amiable companions and Abe took Duke as his example.

Abe's regard for Duke is such he has adopted many of his mannerisms. When Duke sprawls frog-like on the living room rug, so does Abe. When Duke is pleased

with his circumstances he gives off a loud groan signi-
fying his contentment. So does Abe.

Of course, it will be a while, if ever, before Abe is a
retriever of Duke's class. But he has given a good
account of himself in his first test.

He wasn't keen about discipline when the shooting
began at daybreak. The kid was peering into a candy
store, he wanted to go several directions simultaneously,
he tried to retrieve birds for everybody in our hunting
party.

But soon he steadied and gave a fine performance. The
birds were dropping in fields matted with alfalfa. Scenting and retrieving them would be challenging even to a
Lab of Duke's experience. I hoped he wouldn't have
repeated failures and become disheartened.

He was fine. The pup not only found my birds, he
looked after the needs of my bereft friend, Bob Jordan.
Bob felt neglected without Duke. He was like a cowboy
without a horse. Abe, perhaps aware of Bob's discom-
fort, served the two of us and did it gladly.

He heard much praise from the many hunters in the
alfalfa fields, hands reached out to stroke his sleek black
pelt, and he was pleased with himself. We're going to
miss Duke, but maybe Abe will be a worthy successor.

Indian Summer at Christmas

As a hunting trip it was no great shucks. The quail had
departed without leaving a forwarding address. The pigeons were as elusive as UFO's. And the dove, like
prosperous merchants, had gone south for the winter —
to Puerto Vallarta and Acapulco, one presumes.

No matter, it was a grand day in the mountains, with
the streams running and the ponds brimming and the trees
ablaze with color. Abe enjoyed every minute because he
knew, or suspected, this was a Christmas bonus.

It was a day set aside for Christmas shopping and Abe,
hearing the conversation, was sulking under the long

table in the family room. For one reason or another, the talents of a remarkable Labrador Retriever had been shamelessly wasted for two long, dismal weeks. Not one day had passed in the field and Abe was becoming as sensitive as coloratura.

Then the phone rang — Abe wouldn't answer because he was pouting — and a friend named Bob was saying it would be an awful shame to waste a beautiful day, a day late in the quail season, in a city crowded with Christmas shoppers. Bob is very persuasive; he made a compelling argument.

Besides, I can't stand to see a grown dog cry. I got one of the guns out of the cabinet and Abe's eyes fairly shone with pleasure. When Abe is going hunting he becomes so affectionate he creates problems. He presses against me as I move about the house assembling my gear, and did you ever try to put on a pair of boots with a 75-pound dog nuzzling your neck and standing on your feet?

I got the fixings for sandwiches and the plastic water bowl for Abe, and he stretched out in the back seat of the blue Buick and groaned with heady anticipation as we drove across town to collect Bob. Abe's Uncle Bob. His No. 2 pal. They are close because Bob not only understands animals, he speaks their language.

"You know what Abe just said to me?" asked Bob, scratching his friend's ears, "He thinks we're a strange pair of characters. If we had good sense we'd stop this neglect and go hunting every day."

On this day at least we accommodated him. We went back to the old haunts where the coveys had huddled in the brush on other happy occasions, our guns at the ready. But it was a futile quest. When the weather is dry, quail are easy to find because their habits are predictable. Quail are poor tourists. They rarely range more than a mile or so.

But the heavy rains had sent them packing. We hunted carefully, if leisurely, with Abe working back and forth between the two of us, checking every shrub, every clump of grass. Nothing. Not a scent, not a bird calling. Only a few quail tracks on a muddy road.

We paused for lunch and Abe stationed himself at our feet, hungrily eyeing the sandwiches, patiently awaiting a tidbit. Bob broke off part of his sandwich. Abe adjusted the napkin around his neck, ate the provender quickly, then wiped the crumbs from his mouth with a discreet gesture. Then he ate part of my sandwich and went for a romp, arousing a snoozing cottontail.

Abe eyed the disappearing bunny with regret but made no effort to chase him. He has learned that rabbits are not sociably accepted to his class of hunting dog. We've had some arguments about this, and Abe lost. Usually when a rabbit takes flight Abe pretends he doesn't notice. It has something to do with dignity.

But this wasn't to be one of those days when Abe gets a mouthful of feathers. We hunted for hours without firing a shot.

"It looks as though we've run out of country," said Bob, finally. Nevertheless, it was a splendid day. It's been years since I've seen running streams in the back country of San Diego. The Sound of Music Country, lyrics by Junipero Serra.

We packed it in and drove past Lake Henshaw — swollen by the storm from 4,000 acre feet to 15,000 acre feet — and stopped at Warner Springs Guest Ranch to pay our respect to a merry Irishman who runs the place. Tom O'Hara had a football game on the television set and oak logs roaring in the fireplace and a touch of spirits to replenish a weary traveler. The old ranch is a pleasant sight in this season, with its silver tip Christmas trees and the glow from the hearth and the warmth of O'Hara hospitality.

It was a lazy, smoky kind of a day — Indian summer on the eve of Christmas — and the narrow, twisting road leading from Santa Ysabel to Ramona and beyond to San Diego was crowded with city types carrying Christmas trees as we reluctantly turned homeward. Christmas trees and station wagons acrawl with smiling children, and a pox on Scrooge.

We had been hunting for a couple of hours and it wasn't until the heat of day began coming on when my companions began avoiding me. Even my devoted Labrador Retriever, Abe of Spoon River, was keeping a discreet distance between the two of us.

It couldn't be bad breath: Abe doesn't even object to onions. I had showered by dawn's early light and splashed myself with cologne. "Men are so vain," observed the helpmeet, "do you plan to shoot the quail or charm them?"

You can't win answering a question like that, so I let it go. But I was puzzled by the chilly attitude of my companions. If I climbed a ridge, they'd take another. And Abe was neglecting his manners. He's trained to work close to me so the birds won't flush out of range. Now he sneaked through the brush and cactus and decided to be helpful to my pal Bob.

Then I began to notice the odor: the smell of something dead. It had been dead quite a while, and it was ripe. I moved along hastily but, strangely, the odor followed me. This continued for some minutes until I finally realized that we were somehow associated.

An examination of the game pocket on my shooting vest quickly established the reason for my unpopularity.

Out tumbled a deceased quail. Deceased by a week and in very poor condition. It had been hanging in the closet of the guest room. Later, when I explained the problem, the lady occupying the room laughed so hard she was almost hysterical.

"I didn't want to complain," said my mother, "but I was thinking of shortening my visit. It was like sleeping near a sewer."

Still, it's been a grand year for wing shooting. Abe has had so much work he's almost as good as his reputation. He's three years old now, in his prime, and he's as birdy as a field trial champion.

He doesn't point the birds, naturally, because that's not a Labrador's style. But he finds the covey — we always know when he has the scent in his nostrils — and he'll probe until he jumps singles out of the brush.

A quail is an elusive target. He comes out of a bush with an explosion and he disappears quickly. You see him for an instant and he's gone. Abe gives me a strange look when I shoot and miss, and he's more puzzled when I don't react in time to throw the gun to my shoulder and fire.

This is sporty shooting, and in one respect, it's like playing golf or baseball. All of us .200 shooters are subject to hot streaks and slumps. Good days and bad. I get the idea I've finally mastered the art of swinging on a blur of feathers, then I come up empty.

It's a vigorous physical activity. By the end of the day even Abe is footsore and weary. He lies quietly on the back seat of the car on the return trip, content, heavy with sleep. When he's fresh, Abe is restless in a car. He'll nudge the driver and demand that a window be lowered to admit fresh air. Or he'll peer out the rear window, wondering where he's been.

Abe has a handsome head and his eyes are intelligent

and expressive. He is as black as a coal stove. I recall the time we stopped at a service station in Fresno and a small black youngster came over to inspect him. The child regarded Abe with admiration and wonder.

"A mighty fine dog," he said finally, "he don't have a white spot on him anywhere."

Abe even has a black spot on his tongue.

They say a dog is a man's best friend because he never barks at his master. But Abe has other endearing qualities. I like the way he's waiting at the gate to greet me every evening, his head peering over the fence, his eyes warm and eager. Or, if he's in the house, he nudges aside the drapes on the big sliding glass door and stands there silhouetted against the light.

The nice thing about Abe is that he's always ready to go hunting. He can get dressed on a moment's notice and he's not vain about combing his hair. His life is beautifully uncomplicated. No meetings to attend, no columns to write, no books to balance.

Take the shotguns out of the cabinet and Abe starts dancing. Suddenly, the room is too small. Everywhere you go there's a Labrador pushing against you, stepping on your feet, communicating a sense of excitement and urgency.

You beg of him to be patient. "Just take a seat over there," you tell him, "and kindly stay out of my way. We'll be going a lot sooner."

Abe is obedient and dutiful. He sits. But he forgets. A guy leans over to lace a pair of boots and gets a moist, affectionate kiss. Abe sure doesn't feel rejected.

We've had some fine times this winter and we'd like to roll back the date for the close of the quail hunting season in Baja California now that it's less than a week away. Already we miss the fun knowing it's going to happen.

How could anybody be bored during the hunting season?

The first time we encountered Bobby and Wes, the two of them were astride a large horse, riding bareback, Bobby holding the reins and Wes holding firmly to Bobby.

We were exploring for quail in Baja California, creeping gingerly over a rutted and rocky road that scratched against the underside of our low-slung Buick, listening for the birds to betray their whereabouts. Then we met the two boys on the horse and I tried to ask them in pidgin Spanish if we might find quail in the lovely valley.

Bobby regarded me with amusement. "Sure," he said in perfect English, "turn your car around and follow us."

We followed the horse and the boys and two collie dogs for a while and then Bobby reined up beside the road. "The quail are beside the gate," he counseled. "Don't shoot the ponies in the corral." He smiled. "Please excuse us now," he said, "I must go work the cattle."

Bobby has an intimate knowledge of the ranch. We got into the quail right away and had a fine shoot. When we became better acquainted, they showed us a tree where bees are in residence. "If you want honey," said Bobby graciously, "we'll get it for you." And they began hunting with us, picking up empty shells and competing with Abe of Spoon River in retrieving the birds.

Abe might have sulked a bit when we were hunting in cholla cactus, the jumping kind, and that's very hard on a

Labrador Retriever, if he's careless. Luckily, I had my needle nose pliers because Abe came to me with a cactus bulb in his nose, and more of the stuff attached to his left front paw, and that smarts. He stood patiently while the barbs were removed and very carefully thereafter, offering no protest when the boys usurped his retrieving duties.

Once we were walking through a rocky area on the slope of a steep hill, and Wes tugged at my elbow. "This is a dangerous place," he said. I looked about for a few seconds, then jumped off a rock to a lower elevation. Wes followed closely behind me. Then we heard a rattlesnake. The singing of the rattles was so loud it sounded like the whine of a high wire.

I whirled and saw it instantly. Coiled and hostile, about four feet removed. It had the girth of a man's wrist. A red rattler. A species unfamiliar to Abe and, being curious, he went directly toward the snake, intending to investigate. I shouted his name, ordering him to me, and to my vast relief he obeyed. Maybe that constant day-to-day obedience training saved my dog. I shot the rattler and that awful, unnerving sound of rattles finally quieted.

"We almost always see snakes in this place," said Bobby, "We chase them and kill them with rocks." Bobby is 10. His brother, Wes, is 7. They are citizens of the United States who live with their parents on a remote ranch hidden in a picturesque valley of the peninsula. They are fine boys, polite, friendly, high-spirited and excellent company.

Bobby is tall and tireless, Wes is small and ambitious. Those ridges get awful steep and frequent for a 7-year-old boy, but Wes tags along. Once he tangled with an unfriendly cactus and the thorn went through his boot into the foot. I overheard him talking to himself. "Goddamn cactus sure do hurt," he said.

When Wes complained of being weary and footsore. I urged him to go sit in the car for a while. "No," he said, "I don't want to be alone."

It was important that the boys picked up the empty shell casings. They used them in war games. "We fill them with dirt and drop bombs," said Bobby.

The third time we went to the ranch we promised to bring along a .22 rifle as a gift for Bobby. "Hunt on the hill near the house," requested Bobby, "so we'll hear the shooting." They were sitting at the gate when we arrived.

As a gesture of hospitality, they brought us an orange and candy. It isn't easy for a boy to give up his candy, but they offered it cheerfully. After a while we paused for lunch. It was a warm pleasant day, more autumn than winter, and we built a fire in a charcoal brazier in the shade of a large oak tree.

"Will you have some steak?" we asked the boys. "Oh, no thanks, it is yours," said Bobby. But there was plenty for everybody, including the T-bones for Abe, and we had a fine meal. We had bolillos (hard rolls) purchased in the bakery at Rosarito Beach, and salad, and cerveza, and soda pop for the boys. A man could eat a meal like that and slump against a tree and sleep for maybe an hour with no great effort.

But there is no time for siestas for active boys and eager quail hunters. Soon we were climbing the ridges again, puffing and sweating, rousing the birds from the brush. I was wearing one of those bright orange American Airlines golf caps because it shows plainly in the brush. Wes admired it greatly.

"Do you work at a service station?" he asked.

Then darkness came swiftly, ignoring our protests, and we drove the boys back to the ranch house and prepared to depart. It was chilly in the twilight and Wes was shivering. He disappeared into the house and when he returned there were ashes on his nose and forehead. We suspected he had crawled into the hearth for warmth.

We won't be hunting with our new pals for a while because the season has ended. But we'll think of them often, of the good times we had with two boys on a horse.

Last of the Mountain Men

The first time the cactus grabbed me by the trouser legs I used the phrase not heard in the drawing room. One of my hunting companions, Dick McCain, was greatly amused.

"My friend," he counseled, "you have just made the acquaintance of the wait-a-minute bush."

I would rather be tackled by Jack Lambert, the Steelers' linebacker, than a wait-a-minute bush. When Lambert releases you, at least you don't need pliers to remove the thorns.

Those of us who hunt valley or mountain quail in Alta or Baja California have intimate knowledge of the wait-a-minute bush because the birds are perversely fond of cactus. Joseph Wood Krutch, the naturalist, becomes rapturous when describing the beauty of cactus, and I share his enthusiasm — up to a point.

My friend Abe of Spoon River comes whimpering to me with bloodied and aching feet, and I remove the cactus needles and offer expressions of tender sympathy.

Dick McCain is contemptuous. Like Atilla the Hun, McCain expects a hunting dog to ignore pain and play even if injured.

"City dogs," says McCain in a superior tone, "they are soft just like their masters."

It is well to tolerate a certain amount of abuse from McCain, however. He is an authentic mountain man, one of the last of the old breed, and he can lead you to more mountain quail than most wing shooters will encounter in a lifetime.

There have been McCains in the arid, rocky country around Jacumba for nearly a century, and they named a valley there — McCain Valley — for Dick's grandfather, or maybe it was an uncle, who taught him to track a deer or a mountain lion over terrain as hard as flint, and to swear in a dozen languages, and to drive a Jeep where a sure-footed horse would be afraid to go.

One of the pleasures of hunting with McCain is watching him make campfire coffee. He's got this old iron pot, blackened by the smoke of campfires, that probably came west with the Lewis and Clark Expedition, and all he needs is some dry brush and a dry match, a shallow hole in the ground, and fresh coffee.

Pretty soon the water in the old iron pot starts to boil and Dick tosses in the coffee, then he hits it now and then with a cup of cool water until he decides the chemistry is just right.

McCain was insulted when I asked for sugar. "When I make coffee on the campfire," he assured me, "it's sweet as candy."

I wouldn't tell Dick because I wouldn't want to hurt his feelings, but I've had better coffee at the automat. Even a thirsty coyote wouldn't drink it.

But McCain is an agreeable companion, and a fine shot, and a tireless hunter, and he covers more ground than Kojak. His wife and daughters think he should be less ambitious. His back gives him constant pain because a horse fell on him but Dick pretends not to notice.

He went to see a physician in the city and was told he would need an operation. "No sir," said Dick, stubbornly, "nobody is going to cut on me." That being the case, he'd have to wear a brace for his back. Or so the doctor believed.

"Thank you very much for the advice," said Dick, and walked out of the doctor's office. Back at the ranch he took a couple of aspirin, and somehow got on his horse and went looking for his cattle. He shot a fat buck during the season, added some Indian artifacts to his collection, noted the whereabouts of several covey of mountain quail and then took up with a fellow who had a rented helicopter and the two of them camped in the desert for several days.

The helicopter bounced several times before it finally got under way and Dick's wife, LaVon, who doesn't frighten easily, was begging him to get out of that fool machine before he killed himself. She could see Dick laughing and waving when the bird labored into the sky, just clearing a telephone wire and a live oak tree.

When he came back from the desert, the door was latched. LaVon wouldn't permit him to enter the house. Not that she was angry, but Dick hadn't bathed for several days and he was awfully ripe and he was approaching downwind. LaVon gave him a hose and a scrub brush and a can of Old Dutch Cleanser, and told him to bury his clothes when he had made himself presentable.

I would guess Dick knows more about cattle than he does women, though that is true of almost everybody, including dudes from the city who are ignorant about cattle. But he has a sentimental side. When his youngest daughter, Pie, got married he not only gave the union his blessing but welcomed the boy with the most sincere gesture anybody could imagine.

As a wedding gift, Dick presented his new son-in-law with his old cowboy hat, the one with all the cuts and stains and memories of a thousand days and nights on the open range. It's crumpled, misshapen, battered by weather and much use, a very ugly old hat. The boy wears it proudly.

The People at Witch Creek

As we waited for daylight, the coyotes began caroling. We could distinguish three voices, maybe four, a miniature a cappella choir. Boy sopranos rejoicing over the glory of a new day.

"Isn't that a lovely sound?" asked a companion. "It's like waking up to the music of the Vienna Boys Choir."

Our excuse for attending this exclusive concert was the deer hunting season. We go as often as possible, beginning and ending the day in darkness, and if you asked me why, I might say that a phone never rings on a mountain.

But you can walk into Bill Tellam's kitchen before daylight and find him chatting on the phone while he heats the coffee. Tellam raises cattle and sons (four) and hell.

I think of him as the Marlboro Man. Tall, trim, face all planes and angles, among the last of a dwindling species. The authentic cowboy. He's rawhide tough, but without meanness.

Once he said of his third son, John, "You know, it makes me feel sort of proud just to be seen with that boy."

Everybody smiles when Tellam walks down the street in Julian. They know him as Willie but I address him as Bill because when we first met he offered a hand and said, "Hello, I'm Bill Tellam."

I guess that's the name he prefers. I know how his youngest son, Allen, feels about being called Allie. When a boy is old enough to handle a shotgun, he's entitled to some respect. Besides, it's hard being the youngest of four boys.

When the dove hunting season arrived, Allen checked the Tellam weapon inventory and found that Steve, Mike and John had cleaned out the shotguns. But Allen is resourceful.

He got on the phone and called his friend, Harry Holt, also known as Harry the Horse. Harry the Horse is maybe 70 years and some change but he's about the same age as Allen Tellam, 12, in ways that matter.

"Harry," said Allen, "why don't you bring that .20 gauge and we'll shoot some doves?"

He did, and they did.

The Tellams of Witch Creek earn a living from ranching and cattle, but I don't know how they find time. Mostly they are occupied with hunting and football.

Steve, the oldest, is a safety on the Julian High School varsity. Mike, the second son, is a wide receiver and John is the quarterback on the junior varsity.

Considering all the energy and activity of five male creatures, the Tellam household is astonishingly calm and orderly. And that reflects the influence of Eileen Tellam, the attractive lady who shares their company. I suspect she is beyond surprise.

When you've seen one son push another through a window, who needs an encore?

But most of the arguments are good natured and they involve deer hunting and football. A boy with his mind on a trophy buck might forget to feed the calves. And everybody holds strong opinions about football. Especially the Marlboro Man.

"I don't see how a man who has never put on a suit can know so much about football," said John, the quarterback, after receiving the counsel of his father.

It is a happy state of affairs, though hardly a coincidence, that Tellam has the cattle and hunting rights of the most scenic ranches in Southern California and, blessedly, they are still uncorrupted by urban sprawl. We can pass a day without hearing the voice of a stranger, and we often do.

Our companions are bandtail pigeons wheeling in the sky; quail rising in sudden, noisy flight; ducks setting their wings in an east wind; a bobcat drowsing in the sun; a coyote regarding us curiously, and deer. The woods are wormy with deer.

Deer hunting, as I said, is our excuse. We study them through our glasses but seldom disturb them. Each time I return from a day in Tellam's company, I try to explain what it is all about.

"Did you shoot a buck?"

"No."

"Did you see a deer?"

"Yes, lots of them."

"Why didn't you shoot one?"

"Because if I shoot one I'll have to stop hunting."

Now the last day of the season has arrived and the locker is empty, but no matter. It wasn't deer we were hunting, it was solitude and beauty, an escape from tension, and some other things easier felt than explained.

Did you know that in the San Diego back country we are now experiencing spring, winter and autumn all at once? The miracle of rain has brushed the mountain meadows with green, the trees are bright with yellow, gold and red, the colors of autumn; and the wind from the southwest is raw and bitter.

Maybe I can't fully explain what we've been hunting. But one thing I do know: we found it.

I hadn't thought of hunting as a spectacular sport until Mike Connaly invited me to go hawking.

Mike is a master falconer, owner of two sleek peregrines, and the willing captive of a sport which has enchanted mankind for 6,000 years. Men were practicing falconry before they learned to write.

It was agreed my wife and I could witness a duck hunt.

"Choose a day that suits you," said Mike, "hawking is my life. I exist mainly to serve these birds."

That's largely true. Mike constructs his work (he's a carpenter, a framer of houses), his family life and social activities around the hunting schedule of his two peregrines, Witch and Ruby.

"It's not very good for the ego," he noted with a wry grin, "but the falconer is subservient to his hawks. It's my function to see that they have an opportunity to kill something to eat every day. That's about the extent of our tie.

"If I fail them for as much as two or three days, I'm on thin ice."

I began to understand the appeal and the excitement of hawking on a recent morning when we met in the vicinity of Del Mar where, it was hoped, the falcons would have duck for breakfast. Mike arrived in a pickup truck with camper; his companions included two hooded peregrines and a spotted German pointer, Molly.

Molly is useful in getting birds off the water. When a falcon is in the sky, ducks are possessed of fear and caution. The ducks are safe on the water because the peregrine kills by stooping on flying prey. Usually the duck is doomed. A duck might fly at 60 miles per hour, but the peregrine is three times faster.

On this occasion the falconer had observed canvasback ducks swimming and feeding on a small pond at the edge of a golf course. The conditions were right for hawking: lots of open terrain where Connaly could keep his eye on the peregrine and be seen in return.

Mike lifted his prize peregrine, Witch, from the camper, removed her hood, and the falcon perched on his gloved fist. She seemed a noble creature, regal of manner and fierce disposition.

But the female peregrine, with her long scimitar-shaped markings has a disconcerting resemblance to Mike Marshall, the Atlanta Braves' testy, cranky relief pitcher. I kept a discreet distance from the falcon.

The falcon rested on Connaly's fist for a moment, then she was airborne, flying low with quick wingbeats, then gaining altitude. At that instant, I grasped the drama of hawking.

The bird was free of all restraint, wheeling high in the

clear winter sky; if it chose it could fly forever, over the horizon, to the ends of the earth. Mike Connaly had invested six years of training and care in this falcon but the link between man and bird was fragile.

My heart leapt as Witch, distracted by the flight of pigeons, flew beyond the range of my binoculars. Mike stood in the middle of a brown field, calling the peregrine and swinging a lure (a leather strap fitted with duck feathers) to attract the falcon's attention.

Suddenly she came into view again, at first a speck in the sky, then growing larger, flying very fast. Mike ran to the pond nearby and hurled rocks he had stashed in his pockets to startle the indolent canvasbacks.

When the ducks took flight they found themselves in an awful peril. The falcon dropped on one of the canvasbacks but just nicked it and flew on. Then another duck flew madly with the peregrine in furious pursuit. it was a mismatch, but again the duck survived. The falcon missed.

"Maybe she wasn't so hungry, maybe she didn't care enough," shrugged Connaly after the bird returned to his fist and allowed herself to be tied around the legs with straps known as jesses. "They're not perfect; they don't perform the same every day. But I've met my responsibility, I got duck into the sky for her."

Mike Connaly brings devotion to falconry that even critics of the sport would admire. His commitment to the birds is total. I believe I understand the attraction. Every time he goes hawking he experiences suspense and excitement basic to man's nature. A man who has hunted with a falcon most likely would sell his shotguns.

We left the pond where the frightened canvasbacks had sought shelter and drove to a nearby field. It was time for the peregrine, Ruby, to get her daily exercise. She flew from Mike's fist and soon there was a fresh crisis. When Ruby gained altitude, she glimpsed a coyote running in the field, a coyote with a ground squirrel in its mouth.

Ruby stooped on the coyote, demanding that the

animal surrender the ground squirrel. Laughingly, Connaly shirled his lure to attract the falcon's attention. When she responded he released a pigeon from a leather bag.

The peregrine stooped with flashing wings and soon she was feasting on squab. It happens every day in nature, a matchless drama. I shall soon not forget.

Chapter 3

THE DOMESTIC LIFE

The woods are made for the hunters of dreams,
The brooks for the fishers of song;
To the hunters who hunt for the gunless game,
The streams and woods belong.
                                    Sam Walter Foss

Abe is a water dog and I'm an Aquarius, which makes us kindred spirits. We're both becoming fretful about San Diego's version of a monsoon season.

For one thing, it has just about wrecked the quail hunting. The birds are huddled in the brush and the roads in the back country are so mired with mud even a Jeep can't negotiate them. Abe is morose, and his master is surly.

This is our favorite season, the time we practice togetherness. Abe will be curled under an end table in the living room, apparently in a deep, dreamless sleep, when he hears the jangle of car keys on the other side of the house. Instantly, he appears in the door to the bedroom, tail wagging, an expectant expression on his intelligent face.

If the old boy is wearing those faded Levis, and the roughout boots with the lopsided heels, and the dirt-stained cowboy hat, Abe knows the boss is up to something worthwhile. He sniffs the boots and the Levis, hopeful of catching scents of past experiences, and his mood is pure joy.

We walk up the long hallway together, Abe prancing and jumping, and then he surveys the scene with satisfaction while the shotguns are removed from the gun cabinet. Nothing is believable to Abe until his nose tells him it is so. He sniffs the guns and the gun cases; then, convinced, he goes to the door and waits impatiently.

Abe reaches the gate leading from the back yard in about three jumps. Then, minding his manners, he seats himself and awaits permission to go into the outer world where dogs and people find so much excitement. On hunting days, Abe's manners are impeccable. Other times he will seat himself upon command with great reluctance, folding slowly, by degrees, and his eyes mirror annoyance and resignation. On hunting days, he sits without even waiting for the hand signal.

Not this year, though. If it isn't rain it's a football game, or something equally ridiculous, and the dispositions of the dog and his master are rapidly deteriorating. Neither, by nature, is a house animal.

Each morning Abe scratches on the sliding glass door, demanding entrance, as soon as he hears the old boy moving about the house. Sleep replenishes his hope and ambition, and he comes bounding into the living room, his heart full of love, visions of bird shooting dancing in his head.

The old boy is still in his pajamas, clutching a newspaper, but that isn't really discouraging. Lots of times he gets out of his pajamas after a few minutes and puts on something sensible. Like Levis and boots.

The old boy returns to his favorite chair and Abe sits beside him, somehow leaning back without losing his balance, and pressing his head against the master's shoulder. He sighs and makes a noise deep in his throat, denoting bliss. The old boy absently strokes Abe on the head, or scratches his ears, and then becomes absorbed in his newspaper. Abe puts his nose under the arm of his friend, and pushes it upward.

"Pay attention to me," his eyes invite.

Finally, he is satisfied. He excuses himself, then he goes about the house and pays his respects to the other members of the family. If the heir hasn't departed for school, he bounds joyously to the side of his young friend and greets him energetically. And sometimes, wetly.

"Stop licking me on the ear!" the heir protests, indignantly.

Abe is unconcerned. The boy sounds angry but his hands are busy stroking the dog's shiny black hide, and the hands are loving, not angry.

"Abraham," says the boy, solemnly, "you are quite possibly the most handsome Labrador Retriever on the block. I would even go so far as to say you are one of the finest dogs in California, or the entire west."

Abe looks immensely pleased. He struts a bit going across the room where he stations himself before the mistress, gazing lovingly into her face.

"Your breath is terrible," says the lady by way of greeting. "Abe, you should gargle with Listerine."

Abe ignores this insult because the mistress is hugging him, pressing him close to her head.

"Get your tail out of my coffee cup!" protests the lady. She sounds alarmed.

Now Abe is content. Or almost. He somehow situates himself under the end table beside the divan and goes to sleep. Sometimes he snores, and he twitches when he dreams, his legs moving as though he were running. If the dream is unpleasant, he will make little noises of protest or fright.

All the while, though, he is listening for the sound of the car keys. Finally, he hears them and he is waiting there in the door to the bedroom — he's magic, he just materializes — when the old boy turns around.

Alas. No boots, no Levis, no cowboy hat. The old boy is wearing a tie and a white shirt and those other things that have nothing to do with fun. No good ever comes of that. Abe doesn't even bother to accompany his friend to the door. Disgusted, he crawls back under the end table and this time he really sleeps.

Another rainy day...

I knew it was time to get back to work when Abe of Spoon River began snipping the blooms from the orchid cactus.

"That fool dog has been behaving strangely ever since you became ill," said the lady of the house, "but this is too much. We should have named him Ferdinand."

This lady is quite fond of Abraham, but now a tone of irritation edged her voice. The orchid cactus is the Mona Lisa of her little gallery in the west. When the plant blooms she regards it as fondly as found money.

But now the exotic Labrador Retriever was trotting around the patio with the precious bloom clenched between his teeth.

"Why doesn't he chew on bones like other dogs?" asked the lady with devastating logic. "Or he could do something useful, like trimming the hedge."

A classy retriever, Abraham. A retriever with the soul of a poet. He trotted over to the lady and dropped the bloom into her lap. An offering of love.

I was reminded of Bugs Baer's classic line about the

old ballplayer who was thrown out by 10 feet, trying to steal second: "His heart was full of larceny, but his feet were honest."

Abe's pose of innocence failed to deceive the missus.

His mischief was a mild form of protest. For several days his hunting partner had been occupying space in the house and that usually is an encouraging sign to Abe. Often it means a trip into the field for bird shooting and, at worst, a good romp and some work with the training dummy.

This time, however, it was joyless vacation. The master curled up in his bed and slept endlessly, 30 hours at one stretch. They brought him gruel and aspirin and when he roused himself he showed little interest in Abraham.

Once in a while Abe would poke him with his wet nose. Getting no response, he would lie beside the bed and mope.

On the third day, Abe developed a cough. A sympathy cough, his mistress decided.

"Hurry and shake the flu before that flaky dog gets a case of pneumonia," she urged.

She fed the sympathetic Labrador an aspirin hidden in a meat ball. Aspirin tartare. He found it delicious and his eyes appealed for more medicine. But the lady turned him away.

Sad to relate, Abe has a weight problem. Since the wing shooting season ended in February, he hasn't been getting a proper amount of exercise and his stylish silhouette isn't what it used to be.

His pal, Bob, came to call and was more concerned about Abe than the one with the flu.

"Abe," said Bob, shocked, "you're getting fat!" Abe hid behind the big red leather chair in the family room and sulked.

I thought of sending him to the Golden Door, but the lady of the house objected. "Let him drink Metrecal like the rest of us peasants," she declared. Her tone was firm.

As soon as I feel vigorous again, we'll resume our physical fitness program. We go for long, brisk walks and Abe has a grand time sniffing the flowers and exploring the neighborhood. But what he really needs is a speed reading course.

The most effective antidote to boredom is a good library. I went through several books and numerous magazines, acquiring much useless information about Alaska, Israel, Provincetown, Mass., and other garden spots of the world. And I came across an interesting account of author Evelyn Waugh by his brother, Alec.

Evelyn must have been precocious, indeed. At age 11, he told his brother: "My father is a dreadful man. He likes Kipling."

At night, when weary of reading, I would listen to a concert by a mockingbird in the sycamore trees.

Mockingbirds and night people are kindred spirits. Listening to this bird caroling in the soft spring breeze, I was reminded of the impromptu concert Caruso once gave his pal, O.B. Keeler, in a small southern town many years ago. Keeler was a prominent Atlanta golf writer, the Boswell of Bobby Jones, but nevertheless a man of culture. The voice of Caruso was one of his passions and Caruso, in turn, treasured Keeler's friendship.

This was an occasion when the food was superb, and the wine was good and plentiful, and finally the two men returned to the hotel where they were in residence. It was well past the witching hour, but Keeler wanted song, not sleep. He urged Caruso to sing an aria or two in the lobby and the great man agreed.

Caruso mounted the steps to the mezzanine and began singing as though he were center stage at the Met. As usual, he was in magnificent voice. He sang a dozen arias; as his voice filled the hotel other guests, in robes and gowns, began popping out of their rooms, enthralled by this unlikely but wonderful spectacle.

The mockingbird in the sycamore tree is my Caruso.

Southern California's version of autumn approaches on cat feet. The days are still ablaze with sunshine but there is a faint chill in early morning and in the deepening dusk, the best hours for a man and a boy and a dog to walk softly in the woods.

The change of seasons does not seem subtle to the sleek black Labrador, Abe of Spoon River. The aroma of wood smoke is in the air again and he becomes increasingly restive.

He experiences great excitement when the alarm clock chatters before night has retreated and he hears the master clumping about the house, making those early morning noises that are usually a prelude to a hunting trip.

Abe has studied the habits of the old chap very carefully, you see, and he knows he is no competition for the rooster except when the deer are legal game and the birds are on the wing. The master is notoriously grumpy about being awakened at other times of the year, but his disposition improves with the arrival of autumn.

Indeed, he is absurdly cheerful. He gently awakens his teen-age son, peeling back a mound of blankets, and offers the day as a present.

"Remember, son," he says softly, "we're going hunting today."

The boy is heavy with sleep and he frowns at the intrusion. "I'm cold," he says. Then: "Would you bring me orange juice and coffee?" Finally: "All right. I'll be dressed in a minute."

Abe has stationed himself on the stoop outside the door that opens from the patio into the living room, and he presses his ear against the glass, listening intently to the sounds within the house. Every noise has meaning. He hears a click as the gun cabinet is opened, he shivers with anticipation.

But, to Abe, the preparations seem to last endlessly. He becomes impatient. He scratches at the door, counseling haste. He would like to bark but he is much too mannerly for such crude behavior. He whines instead, and the sound becomes increasingly shrill until the boss comes out of the house, scratches the dog's ears, and speaks reassuringly.

Abe is momentarily comforted. He sniffs at the master's worn roughout boots and the stained Levis; the familiar odors give him a sense of security. These are the symbols of the good life. Abe vibrates with happiness. His wagging tail expresses his pleasure. Abe presses his fine black head against the legs of his companion. There is a splendid rapport here.

Yet the relationship is imperfect, flawed by problems of communication. Abe's instinct is unerring in the field but he sometimes misreads the signs of city living. He fails to grasp the simple fact that the schools again are in session and that the early morning sounds within the house have nothing whatever to do with a man, a boy and a dog going hunting.

A dog, like a man, relates to his own experience. If the boss is up while the city sleeps, the day has made a promising start. Often he feels betrayed. The old chap has aroused himself, not so cheerfully this time, for the prosaic purpose of getting the heir off to school.

Abe hears the noises, sees the lights wink on, and visualizes a romp in the hills. But the man and the boy ignore him. He scratches at the door and the whine in his voice becomes insistent.

Finally, the boss opens the door and he is not wearing boots or Levis, and his manner is unfriendly.

"Forget it, Abe," he says crossly, "we're not going hunting today."

Abe reacts as though he has been slapped. He lowers his head and slinks to his favorite corner in the patio, concealing himself under a camellia bush. He stretches out on his stomach, against the dark soil, trying to make himself inconspicuous. He is one with the earth.

Later the old boy returns to the patio with a newspaper and a mug of coffee and sits for a while in a deck chair, shading the newspaper from the morning sun. Abe emerges hesitantly from beneath the camellia bush and nudges the boss under the arm, spilling some of the coffee.

The boss doesn't seem to notice. He continues reading and he strokes Abe's black head, and the dog presses against him.

That's why we're such good friends, I guess. We hold no grudges.

But Where Are the Feathers?

These are truly the dog days for my pal, Abe of Spoon River.

Spring is upon the land. Soft clouds float across a shiny sky, the meadows are ablaze with wildflower, and the woods trill with birdsong.

But all of this glory holds no charm for a Labrador Retriever. He accepts gladly when invited to go fishing but it isn't the same, you understand, as watching tensely while a flight of pintail set their wings, or reacting to the explosion of a covey of quail in matted brush.

Abe goes fishing for the same reason some wives accompany their spouses to baseball games. It relieves the monotony. But he wonders about the merit of an activity where the prey doesn't wear feathers.

He sits quietly in the boat while his companions cast for bass and he displays a flicker of interest when a fish is netted and placed on a stringer. He pokes his head over the side of the boat and watches curiously while the bass thrashes about on the stringer. But it's a poor substitute.

The best moment of the day comes at sunset when we hear the sweet, pure call of a valley quail from a distant hill. Abe becomes very alert and attentive. Later, as we glide to the shore, a covey of birds whirs from the brush and Abe is ecstatic. He has to be restrained from leaping from the boat. His nose is full of delicious scent and he trembles with excitement.

"That," says a friend named Bob, "is to remind us of the joys of autumn."

"Hurry, October," says the message in Abe's eyes, "do not tarry along the way."

Finally, the approaching darkness and the chill evening wind encourage us to leave the lake. As we make the boat secure at the dock there is a considerable splash, the sound of body meeting water, a bellybuster. Now that it is time to leave, Abe is ready for a swim.

It is in the natural order of things that no Labrador can enter a car with a dry coat. Asking Abe to stay out of the water is like asking Howard Cosell to take a vow of silence. It wouldn't be much of a trip home if he couldn't drip water on the upholstery and lean lovingly against a companion. He is affectionate, but untidy.

But, first, there is the ceremony of shaking himself. His black pelt is heavy with moisture as he rises from the lake and walks carefully, trying not to spill a drop, to one who is bent over his fishing gear. Then Abe shakes himself. It is an experience something like walking into a lawn sprinkler fully dressed.

This is sometimes followed by some highly imaginative cussing.

"You remind me," says Bob, "of the fellow who always called a spade a spade until he tripped over one in the dark."

Abe ignores this poor effort at humor.

Actually, little escapes his attention. Recently, for example, it was decided within the family council to acquire a station wagon on the premise that this is a functional vehicle for people who hunt and fish and keep company with a large, black Labrador. Abe would have his own quarters in the rear and we even carpeted the floor to make him comfortable.

A grand idea. Abe could observe the passing scene through three picture windows and in no time at all he became familiar with the details of this glistening new machine. On the day of the fishing trip, Abe waited impatiently in the station wagon while his friends had coffee in Bob's apartment.

"Why don't I invite Abe to join us?" asked Bob, and he went to the car to release him. Soon the two returned and Bob was laughing.

"I feel like a fool," he said sheepishly, "Abe had to show me how to open the door to the wagon."

He had gone around trying all the doors and finding them locked. Meanwhile, Abe was endeavoring to get his attention. Catching Bob's eye, he would go to the rear door and press his nose against the window just above the door handle. Finally, Bob understood.

"Abe could see it was the only unlocked door," said Bob. "He was doing his damndest to get my attention." If Abe hadn't gotten into retrieving, he might have been a mechanical engineer.

A Shadow Among Shadows

It was sometime during the night when the lady of the house stepped on Abe of Spoon River and capsized.

This disturbed both her equilibrium and her equanimity. "I tripped over your fool dog and almost broke my lovely neck," she said, waking me from a sound sleep.

How do you wake up talking? My mouth was full of cotton, and I resented the interruption of a beautiful dream. Something about winning the Nobel Prize for literature.

Immediately my tone became defensive. "What about Abe? Did you examine him for bruises and contusions? How would you like to wake up with a foot in your ear?"

Abe sleeps in the long hallway of our scatter, guarding the bedroom door. He is a large, black Labrador Retriever, noble of spirit, and difficult to see in a hazy light. He's a shadow among shadows.

"Why can't he sleep outside like other dogs?" asked the lady in an aggrieved tone. She was rubbing a bruised knee after colliding with a night table. The level of noise was several decibels too high for comfort.

I was appalled. "But he's not JUST a dog. He's a member of the family. He is loyal, courteous and kind. He is your faithful and devoted guardian. His sense of duty is sublime."

Silently, I congratulated myself. Those were truly soaring phrases, I thought, for a guy who had been crudely awakened from deepest sleep.

Abe of Spoon River is almost perfect, but I will admit he has one flaw. He snores. I wonder about his dreams. Sometimes he makes little yelping noises and his legs begin working as though he were in full flight. He even barks in his sleep, a breach of manners he would never permit while awake.

He's a quiet fellow, and he cheerfully endures the eccentric behavior of man. At certain times of the year his best friend disappears for long periods, strangely and unaccountably, going off to baseball training camps and golf tournaments and the like. But Abe never whimpers. He just waits and waits and waits.

Abe is sensitive and acutely aware. When his friend calls home from Florida, Abe presses close to his mistress, eavesdropping as best he can.

"It's strange," says the lady of the house, "but he pays no attention when anybody else calls. He must know from the tone of my voice."

I tell her this is very useful information. If Abe begins eavesdropping on other conversations, well...

Abe is extra vigilant when the head of the household is absent. Some nights he scarcely seems to sleep at all. He feels his responsibility.

"I appreciate his devotion," says the spouse, "but he makes me nervous. I go to the kitchen during the night and he'll be sitting there, staring out the window. Either that, or he won't stay in the house at all. He lies on the porch, watching the gate. Then he sleeps all day."

Abe is a very good friend. And his life is beautifully uncluttered. He is available at all hours to go bird hunting and, unlike my other friends, he doesn't have to hurry back for a social doing or beg off because the court clerk has arranged the docket.

Just get the gun out of the cabinet, and Abe is ready.

Abe has sharpened my sense of hearing. He is part of the night sounds of our house. I awaken instantly if my son gets up during the night or if he rolls on his bed against the wall. And I am attuned to the echo of Abe's toenails on the bedroom floor. He makes a clicking noise, like a tap dancer.

Sometime before dawn he is sure to inform me he needs a bit of fresh air. At first, he would stand beside the bed and stare at me, and I would feel his presence. Then he nuzzled me with his cold nose. After that, I began hearing his footsteps and walking quickly.

Abe can hear an ice box door open at a distance of three miles. I go to the kitchen soon after arising each morning and remove a can of tomato juice; instantly there is a sound of scratching on the big sliding glass door. I ignore him for a time, and the scratching becomes more insistent.

"I think," says the spouse, looking up from her newspaper, "that a friend of yours is trying to get your attention."

Somehow I doubt he feels neglected.

There's Beer on His Breath

It was about the time I left Abe behind during a bird shooting trip to northern California that he began tippling.

I tried to explain there wasn't much space in the cabin and, besides, the plane would be heavily loaded. Nevertheless, he became very sulky. He watched the guns and the boots being loaded into the station wagon and he trembled with anticipation.

He was hurt and bewildered when we drove away without him, but I didn't realize the extent of his depression until we returned.

"Your dog has been into the beer," said my wife by way of greeting. I recognized the tone. This beautiful Labrador Retriever becomes exclusively mine when he eats the blossoms off the orchid cactus, digs in the flower beds, becomes too chummy with the resident skunks, or otherwise gets into mischief.

"Beer! What beer?"

"The beer I put under the hedge around the patio to get rid of the snails. It was in pie tins, and Abe drank it. You should get a whiff of his breath."

I let it pass. After all, he's not a problem drinker and I was a bit unsteady myself after the flight from Stockton. A soft rain had fallen throughout the night and most of the morning at Venice Island and our pilot, Bill Black, was uneasy about the condition of the landing strip.

"We might skid right off the runway on the takeoff," said Black. "Maybe it would be smarter to leave the plane here and go home on a commercial flight."

That seemed an eminently sensible course, but I kept my views to myself. I had trust in Black; I knew him to be a fine pilot, greatly experienced, a sane and sensible man as well. When we finished shooting, he directed Roberto, of the Venice Island staff, to drive us over the landing strip in a Jeep.

The strip is mud with a coating of oil, and it was squishy under the tires. The Jeep left ruts as we splashed through little pools of standing water.

Black made his decision. "The strip is OK, we'll leave on schedule."

We cheered the pilot. For one thing, he's lucky. We'd had a marvelous shoot in the morning, easily bagging our limits, while the hunters in other blinds around the island came away empty. Our blind had all the action. I was even more impressed when Black brought down two ducks with one shell.

It was the first time I had seen a Scotch double with ducks. But one should expect economy from a banker, I suppose. We had a grand time, shooting in the gentle rain, and then we went back to the clubhouse to dry ourselves and feast on a lunch prepared by the club chef, Kurt Zerres. Black listened to the weather reports on the aeronautical band of a transistor radio.

"There's a solid front all the way to Bakersfield," said the pilot. "It should be an interesting flight."

The word is hairy. I buckled myself into the plane and tried to appear nonchalant.

"Why are you making the sign of the cross?" asked Keene Wolcott, across the aisle.

Keene's father, Earl Wolcott, took the co-pilot's seat and read the checklist to the pilot. The elder Wolcott is unaccustomed to the luxury of a twin Commander. He's an Alaskan bush pilot and his usual vehicle is an egg-beater.

"It's no sweat, the strip is in good shape," said the gentleman from Alaska cheerfully.

Suddenly we were churning down the runway in a shower of water and mud. The runway was as slick as grease, the plane was sliding, and it seemed we were about to veer off into a cornfield. Not a pleasant sensation. Then Black lifted the machine into the air and we rose above a dike that holds back the San Joaquin River.

I guess my color wasn't very good at that point. Keene Wolcott reached for a jug of Chivas Regal.

"How about a drink?" he asked kindly.

"Make it a double: It's nine o'clock in London."

Then we had another and maybe more to make the weather smoother en route home. After a while we decided it was a beautiful flight. Black made a gentle touchdown in the twilight at Montgomery Field, thus ending what we now considered a perfect day.

I expected Abe to growl when I presented myself at home with limits of ducks and pheasants, but he sniffed me cordially and gave me a silly grin. The influence of the beer, no doubt.

He has this way of sitting on the stoop of the patio and staring accusingly through the glass door, and I used to feel guilty because I thought he longed to share my company.

Actually, I discovered, it's the Persian rug in the entry hall that makes his heart beat faster.

It's a poor little thing, that rug. My wife bought it a few years ago after answering a classified advertisement and it is rather worn from foot traffic. But it is a cherished possession to Abe of Spoon River. The rug is his security blanket.

We became aware of Abe's possessive attitude toward the rug when my wife fell victim to the spring house-cleaning fever. She gets a certain glint in her eye and you know there's going to be a fit of scouring and waxing and polishing. This time she was so thorough she gathered up the rug from the hallway, carried it to the patio, and attacked it with a foamy cleanser.

Abe regarded her with dismay. Abe of Spoon River is a Labrador Retriever, black as coal, not a spot on him anywhere unless you count his gray chin whiskers, and he is the soul of courtesy. He is so polite he will interrupt a meal if you care to make small talk, so fastidious he won't eat food spilled on the ground. But he is sensitive about the rug.

He watched with alarm when the lady snatched up his rug, spread it over a table in the patio and began scrubbing with the cleanser. Abe has a very expressive face, he is largely without guile, and he didn't try to hide his concern. He circled warily about the rug and the table, his brow wrinkled with worry, his big eyes anxious.

The lady tried to console him. She put the brush and the cleaner aside and dropped to her knees to hug his neck. "Don't carry on like that," she urged, "soon you will have the rug again and it will be nice and clean. It will be worthy of one so handsome as you."

Usually her sweet talk is irresistible. Abe is so enchanted he collapses at her feet in a near faint. But this time he sulked. He was suspicious, his manner was chilly. And it seemed his fears had been confirmed that night when he was admitted to the house and the rug remained on the patio.

The entry hall, where we often stumble over Abe's shadowy form, was bare and forbidding. Abe took up his usual station but he was glum. When a member of the family approached he'd open one eye but his tail would not thump in recognition.

We made an effort to appease him. I got the other little Persian rug, another bargain from the classified section, and carried it from my study into the hall. Abe regarded it with disdain. Deliberately, he stretched out beside the rug and pretended to sleep. I know he was faking because Abe snores when he's really asleep; he snores even when he hasn't been into the beer my wife feeds to the snails.

For a dog, he's awfully complicated. He pouted until we finally got the rug back into the hall.

That rug seems to give him sensuous pleasure. He lies there, stretching and yawning, the picture of a dog at peace. When the dinner hour approaches and there is activity in the kitchen, he assumes a watchful attitude. He lies on his stomach, his chin on the rug, his eyes lively and aware. He is secure again; the crisis has passed.

A Labrador Retriever has a hide a seal would envy. He sheds water with ease. He can withstand severe cold and he is the perfect companion in foul weather when there are ducks or geese to retrieve. But Labs have a streak of contrariness; they cheerfully reconcile themselves to the cruelest temperatures during the hunting season, but they are as delicate as toy poodles in the environment of a city.

One begins to hear familiar words: "Oh, how you have spoiled that dog." But the one who says it is a fraud. I come home in the evening and Abe is in the house. "Well," she says, "I can't leave him outside, not with that bad cough."

I wonder if the cough is a cough of convenience. I never hear it when we're bird hunting.

The Dog Who Learned to Bark

I am depleted in strength, but richer in knowledge. For example, I have learned that Montezuma holds me personally responsible for acts of aggression against Mexico and his revenge is fearful.

On the second day, I suspected I was a terminal case. Not that anybody would tell me anything. But my son wouldn't even approach the bedroom and my four-legged friend, Abe of Spoon River, came to my side wearing a hospital mask.

The mere fact that Abe was granted entry to the bedroom was a disturbing portent. There are certain areas of the house where Abe is persona non grata and the bedroom, heretofore, was inviolate. He is a great hunting dog, but personal hygiene isn't his long suit. He sheds. Wherever Abe goes, he leaves a trail of black hair.

Now, suddenly, he was welcome in the master bedroom. He came bounding up the stairs at the invitation of the resident nurse.

"You have a visitor," she announced cheerfully, "but don't send him searching for a cask. He doesn't work for the Red Cross."

Abe came very close and thrust his handsome head into my chest. His nose was damp against my skin. I rubbed his ears and stroked his head and he groaned with delight. The more I rubbed, the louder became the sounds in his throat. Finally, he just dissolved. By degrees he collapsed on the floor and went to sleep, his chin on one of my slippers.

As it developed, this was Abe's reward for mastering a new trick. I thought Abe might be followed into the bedroom by a priest. But, no, the mistress of the house explained, Abe's presence had nothing to do with my delicate health. He had earned the privilege. Abe had learned to bark.

I can anticipate the reader's reaction: what is so remarkable about a barking dog? After all, Abe is six years old and he is said to be an animal of high intelligence. Even retarded dogs can bark.

But Abe just isn't a gabby sort. He would regard Calvin Coolidge as a blabbermouth. A wonderful, loving companion is Abe of Spoon River. A superb hunter of birds. But we had not thought of him as a guardian of the premises. The neighbors knew him as the dog who never barked. They marveled at his restraint.

Then he met Lady B. Good. Naturally, it was a female who changed him. Lady is a feminist. Lady demands to be heard. She raises her voice at cats, people, birds, anything that moves.

Lady is Abe's new girl friend and, naturally, she is trying to improve him. She doesn't believe you can't teach an old dog new tricks.

Abe is a changed retriever. His new personality expressed itself while I was in Mexico City recently on a research project. I learned a lot about bad ice. Meanwhile, Abe was taking on an extra dimension.

This was revealed one evening when the mistress heard a strange sound. It was a dog barking near the house. A dog with a deep bass voice. Very impressive.

The lady was puzzled. She thought: "Who can that be? I've never heard that dog before."

The barking continued, growing louder in volume. A very fierce dog had come into the neighborhood. A dog to be approached with care. Finally, the lady investigated.

It was Abe. Good old Abe, raising merry hell. A glorious sound.

"Shut up, dog!" called a youthful voice from a nearby residence.

Abe turned up the volume. He barked with a rich, throaty roar. He even growled a bit. The lady was thrilled.

She called Abe into the house and hugged him warmly. She pressed her face against his cheek and stroked his fur. It was a tender scene.

"My beautiful, wonderful Abraham," she exclaimed, "at last I have a watchdog."

Naturally, Abe appreciated the attention. Especially when the lady invited him into the kitchen and presented him with a bowl of ground meat.

Abe isn't accustomed to such cuisine. For raw hamburger, he would sing like a canary. And he does. Abe is like an old pitcher who adds a few years to his career by mastering a new technique. Now he growls and barks at alien sounds and his mistress thinks he's charming.

Come to think of it, Abe had good reason for his silence all those years. Till he met Lady, he never had much to bark about.

The skunks leave their footprints in the dust beside Abe's water pan and toward midnight, when the house is quiet, they are emboldened to investigate the patio.

They aren't house pets, you understand, but they are welcome so long as they eat the grubs in the yard and exist peacefully with animals, birds, and people who share the premises. Our skunks are fat and hairy and, usually, non-belligerent.

They display temper (or alarm) only when they detect the scent of Abe of Spoon River on the shrubbery. This isn't very flattering to old Abe. Even at his worst, when he's been digging in the flower beds and his nose is powdered with dust, Abe likes to believe he is more careful about personal hygiene than a skunk.

But, obviously Labrador Retrievers are not highly regarded in the society of skunks. The skunk gets a whiff of Abe and his bushy gray tail stands at attention. Fortunately, Abe is snoozing under a desk in the study and his legs kick occasionally and he growls in his throat as he dreams of quail rising and guns exploding and men shouting and laughing.

Abe no longer invited the company of skunks. When he was youthful and innocent he was curious about the creatures who share his terrain. He approached them in a friendly spirit and was puzzled by their aggressive manner. From this encounter, Abe came away smelling like a sewer.

Now he will cross the street to avoid anything that raises such a stink. If a skunk calls a greeting, Abe pretends not to notice.

Yet the skunks are less of a concern to Abe than a pair of mockingbirds who lately have established residence in a pepper tree that shades the patio.

The mockingbirds are militant and they attack without provocation. They don't seem to realize that Abe poses no threat to songbirds, even songbirds who plagiarize the material of other vocalists.

These are ill-tempered birds. They harass poor Abe as he lies dozing in the afternoon sun and send him scurrying for shelter. He's middle-aged now, working on a paunch, but he moves with surprising agility when the mockingbirds dive at him, shrieking like fish wives. Abe hurdles a hedge and crouches under a low-hanging limb of the pepper tree.

He is resentful of this intrusion, and I am no less indignant. The mockingbird is a thief. He steals the songs of other birds and claims them as his own. He is an imitator. The mockingbird is in a class with the people who introduce talent on TV shows.

Pointers, the late Fred Allen termed them. It was Allen's idea that you could smear the actors with meat and a dog could perform the same role.

In my travels, I often encounter the human version of mockingbirds. These are the people who return to a hotel room at midnight and turn their TV sets to full volume for the late movies. The mockingbird doesn't get an urge to sing until I am in need of sleep.

The mockingbird is enchanted with the sound of his voice. He should be arrested for disturbing the peace. He does more to promote insomnia than black coffee, night baseball or domestic arguments. I have a strong impulse to throw an old shoe at him; that, indeed, would be a comment on his performance.

Instead, I put a pillow over my head and shut out the sounds of the night. When sleep finally comes, I dream that Squeegee is eating the mockingbirds for dinner.

Squeegee is a splendid Siamese cat who belongs to the neighbors and, now that we are acquainted, he is very congenial. He likes people, dogs, cars and he has a great hunger for birds. Often I find him sitting in the front seat of our station wagon, dozing in the sun. The rest of the time he crouches on the high redwood fence that shelters the patio or conceals himself beneath the bird bath in the backyard.

When I see Squeegee on the fence I think of him as a politician. But he isn't really trying to straddle an issue. Squeegee's ambition is to catch a mocking bird or a mourning dove in an unguarded moment and placate his hunger. He works with great stealth, he has enormous patience, and he is unfailingly optimistic. Even if he was oh for four yesterday, he comes to the patio early for special batting practice.

We live in the city but we share our scatter with small wild creatures and this provides a pleasant illusion of being in touch with nature. We can hear the jets roaring on takeoff at Lindbergh Field but we can also hear a mourning dove cooing in a Eucalyptus tree near the bedroom window.

It was a very special occasion when a pair of doves built a nest on a trellis over the dining room window and established residence. We took a paternal interest when the nest became a maternity ward and it was a grievous disappointment when the female laid only one egg, then abandoned it.

That's how doves deal with population control.

The Stick Taps a Message

As I recall, it was the third day after we had returned

from the British Isles that my friend Abe of Spoon River decided he would forgive me. He had felt neglected during our absence, and it did seem a long while because we were away for five weeks.

Abe was sullen. Ordinarily, he rushes to the door and waits expectantly, tail wagging furiously, when he hears the jingle of car keys. Now he avoided me. Forgiveness didn't come easily.

Naturally, he came to my side when I called him. This wasn't a strike, just a domestic spat. But his manner was aloof. He allowed me to stroke his black pelt, but he didn't press against me or extend a paw in greeting. He tolerated me.

Though he had excellent care, he resented being placed with relatives. I learned from my daughter that he had barked night after night in a great roaring voice, disturbing the peace, and arousing all the other dogs in the area. This was his form of protest. It wasn't that he demanded better treatment; he felt deprived.

The racket was uncharacteristic of Abe. He has the civility of an Oxford don. All who know him speak of his gentlemanly ways. He makes you feel good because he finds so much joy in life.

He doesn't even complain when the neighborhood cats enter the yard. He is not cursed by jealously. When he snoozes in a corner of the house he becomes one with the shadows. Only the occasional sound of his collar chain reveals him. And sometimes he snores.

The volume of his snoring makes me wonder if he's been into the liquor cabinet. Or maybe he has a sinus condition. I don't understand how he can make so much commotion with his mouth closed. He sleeps in the position of a lizard, with his chin against the floor. When you approach him, he opens one eye. If you speak to him his long tail begins to move in a sweeping motion. Sometimes the tail is hazardous. We don't position anything fragile on the coffee table.

He hasn't barked since we were reunited and, finally,

he has stopped brooding. Abe isn't the sort to carry a grudge. After ignoring me for two days, he began to make overtures of friendship. I'd come home at the end of the day and Abe, knowing the sound of the station wagon, would be waiting for me at the gate. I could hear him making those little whining noises as I came up the sidewalk and he'd be dancing, unmindful of the flower beds, by the time I reached the door.

Now he's cheerful again. I haven't been able to explain why he couldn't fly on the 747, and there's no point of telling him he wouldn't have liked the movie anyway. Friends don't ask. We're close again and he still thinks I can't work at my desk in the study unless he's parked at my feet. The ash walking stick I brought home from England is a new symbol of pleasure.

Indeed, the stick has a way of appearing in the living room before I really need it. Not that Abe brings it to me. My son is 19 now but he still likes to take long walks in the evening and he uses the walking stick as bait.

The way it works, I'll be relaxing after dinner with coffee and snifter of brandy and suddenly the young man is beside me with an invitation to go walking. It's a pleasant evening, he is saying, ideal for a stroll.

Now I am torn. The couch is comfortable, the brandy is delectable, I'm feeling lazy and there's a book I've been reading. But the walks are pleasurable, too. The boy and I do a lot of talking along with the walking; we stay in touch, and I cherish these moments.

I compromise. Pretty soon, I tell him. Wait just a little. Let me finish my coffee. The boy knows me pretty well. He smiles and says OK and disappears for a while. When he returns he hands me the walking stick. If I am engrossed in the book, he taps the stick lightly on the floor. Abe knows the sound.

He is sleeping or so it seems, because the sound of snoring drifts into the living room. Then he hears the tap,

tap of the stick and—swish!—he's parked before the door, tail wagging. Out we go into the night, a dog straining against a leash, two sticks tapping against the pavement.

The leash is demeaning to such a noble animal, but necessary. Labrador Retrievers are uncommonly intelligent but they have no fear of automobiles. They trust cars as they trust people, and their trust is misplaced. Thus, in safety, we investigate the flowers and shrubs while we discuss the great and small issues of the day. We regard the changing light of evening with wonder and my son, who is knowledgeable about such things, tells me the location of the planets in the sky and where the moon will be tomorrow night and the next.

A nice arrangement, I think. A man and a boy and a dog strolling together on a fine summer evening all on good terms.

Chapter 4

ON THE TRAIL

I never lost a little fish — yes, I am free to say
It was always the biggest fish I caught that got away.

Eugene Field

PUERTO VALLARTA—First of all, we had to ford
the river in the Jeep and the current was swift and just a
bit treacherous. I do not wish for this to seem a dramatic
experience. But it was unusual for a gringo.

The night was as black as a pirate's heart when we
came to the river. We were en route to a lagoon where
Jack Cawood had promised some sporty duck hunting,
and crossing the river was a routine experience for Jack.
He knew the deep places where the Jeep might disappear
in the event the driver miscalculated, and he called out
directions while Dick Grihalva wrestled the wheel and
fretted about his auto insurance.

I thought it was a bad omen when water came through
the floorboard, soaking my shoes, but Grihalva reassured
me. This is a standard procedure for all those who travel
any distance out of Puerto Vallarta on the road to
Guadalajara. The road does a lot to promote business for

the Mexicana Airline. It is in such terrible condition that the usual motoring time between Guadalajara and Puerto Vallarta is 13 hours.

On this day, however, we were fortunate. We weren't going far and we had the good luck to share the company of Cawood, a large, good-humored and fearless man who owns a hotel on the beach because it enables him to be close to good hunting and fishing.

Cawood's philosophy of life is uncomplicated. He tries to go hunting every morning and he seldom allows business to intrude. "I don't have any deadlines to meet," he said as we were departing, "it will be all right if we return by New Year's Day."

Some people regard Jan. 1 as the day when the new year begins. To Cawood, it is the occasion of Grihalva's annual party. Anybody who gets out of bed in three days concludes the party was a failure.

Cawood is always in high spirits but he was content this morning because his hotel, Playa de Oro, was booked to capacity and both the guests and the animals were behaving. At various times his pets have included a wild boar, an ocelot, and a jaguar.

He was especially fond of the wild pig, a sow named Josefina. The ocelot was eliminated when it mistook a guest for a teething ring. Josefina was popular until she upset seven tables and 28 guests one evening while chasing a dog that had wandered innocently into the dining area.

A pig in the dining room isn't considered good form even in Puerto Vallarta, which regards ceremony as nonsense. But a wild pig grunting and slashing at a frightened dog, upsetting tables, terrorizing women and causing men to turn pale, isn't recommended for business. Reluctantly, Cawood gave Josefina to a native.

Now his only pets are two pregnant cats and a Labrador Retriever with a curly tail and a splayed foot, the foot being the result of an accident and the failure of the doctor to set a broken bone properly. In the absence of a veterinarian, Cawood took Negro, as he calls the dog, to a physician and he gladly treated the patient. However, the physician since has become more selective.

Now the town is full of gringos, the gringos pay better than animals, and the physician no longer has time for dogs. Not even purebreds.

Cawood's idea of exciting sport is to toss a spear into a giant manta ray and permit the thing to drag him about Banderas Bay, and this he does often to accommodate television cameramen and magazine photographers. He is the father of two daughters and a beautifully-behaved 10-year-old son named Steve, and the husband of a spirited and attractive Peruvian lady named Teresa. Teresa is resourceful. She loves to attend the cinema, for example, but the theater in Puerto Vallarta is besieged with odors which would offend Josefina, much less Teresa. Teresa solves this problem by taking along a large bottle of cologne and sniffing it frequently. I think she can do almost anything except pronounce the name "Sherlock Holmes." This is too much for a Peruvian. But I digress. I was going to describe the duck hunting but people interest me more than birds, and Cawood interests me more than most people. The hunting was fine. Cawood stationed us on a point and the birds came into the decoys, flock after flock, and there was duck on the hotel menu that evening.

The Labrador, Negro, proved an unreliable retriever but this was not a problem. We had contracted for the services of two native guides—"faithful native guides," Cawood termed them—and they brought back all the wood ducks shot by Grihalva and me. We took a considerable number, including several doubles, and I don't know when I've had a more wonderful day.

It will be fun to get up tomorrow, amigos. Then we go pigeon shooting.

It was a beautiful wedding cake, but it smelled of fish. The bride, lovely Chayito, sniffed the three-tiered confection and then retreated in haste.

"Don't worry, Chayito, the cake will make a fine bait," they reassured the bride, "it will catch a dolphin or a rooster fish tomorrow."

I will try to explain about the cake. It had been in the freezer at Club Aereo Mulege while Chayito and her groom, Harrison Evans, honeymooned in the States. Their wedding had been the big social event of the season in the Mexican community of Mulege, located about midway up the Baja peninsula on the Gulf of California. Chayito and Harrison had postponed the ceremony of the cake until after the honeymoon, and now a small group of friends were gathered for the occasion.

For seven weeks the cake had been in the freezer, keeping company with the cabrilla, pargo, dolphin and other seafood caught in the gulf. The cake looked splendid—Chayito herself had baked it with loving care—but association with the fish gave it a bad reputation. Friends of the bride and groom assembled under the stars on a warm summer night to admire the cake. It was easier to admire the cake than to eat it.

The goom proved his devotion to Chayito by taking a bite of the cake.

"It is really a magnificent cake," said the groom, holding a piece aloft, "only the icing tastes of fish. Won't everybody join me?"

There were no volunteers. The wedding cake looked fine, but it smelled terrible. It sat there, like a dolphin with white icing, and the groom eyed it morosely.

"I guess we will take it home with us," he said, finally. Nobody offered to help. Not even Chayito.

I write this morning of Mulege and the fishy wedding cake because I am just returned from a restful week at my favorite Mexican hideaway. The words form slowly because I have adjusted myself to the pace of Mulege, and this is a world without deadlines. It is a world without newspapers, television sets, clocks and calendars, and the part I like best is the afternoon siesta.

Mulege—pronounced Mool-A-Hay—is only 500 miles below the border and captain Francisco Munoz gets there in about two and one-half hours. In the time of a good siesta Munoz flies his Lockheed Lodestar from Tijuana to Mulege and the clock is turned back two centuries.

Francisco makes the round-trip flight three times each week, alighting his sturdy craft on a clearing in the desert with the touch of a feather, and soon we are in the company of good friends. We come at the invitation of Louis Federico and Don Johnson, the Americans who manage Club Aereo, and we are pleased to see familiar faces—Saul, the bartender; Gilberto Yee, the Chinese-Mexican cook, and others.

At breakfast one morning there was an interesting dialogue between Louis Federico and his pretty young wife, Lana.

"Did you feed the raccoon last night?" asks Louis.
"Yes."

"Did you feed the parrot?"
"Yes."

"Well," says Louis, "You won't have to feed the raccoon or the parrot this morning."

"Why not?"

"Because," says Louis, "the raccoon ate the parrot."

Lana goes to investigate, and soon she returns with three brightly-colored tail feathers.

This is the good, easy life for the gringo visitor to Mulege. Each morning the sports fishing boats go out into the bay in pursuit of dolphin, roosterfish and less glamorous species. Pargo hit the lure almost as quickly as it enters the water and the action is enlivened by a school of playful porpoise.

We swim in the warm clear water of the gulf and there is one glorious day when we take the 32-footer to the Bay of Conception and dig clams for the evening meal. We dive from the boat into the water and soon we have loaded two buckets with clams, and we are thankful the rest of the world has not yet discovered this beautiful bay with its dazzling white beaches.

In the United States, the Bay of Conception would be as crowded and soiled as Miami Beach. In Europe, it would be the French Riviera. In Baja California, it is lovely and unspoiled — not a beach umbrella on 25 miles of sand.

We watch an orange moon hanging like a decoration over the bay, casting its glimmering rays on the gentle swells of the water, and we are content. An old man shuffles along the road by the river, balancing the weight of two buckets of water with a stick across the shoulders; lights from shrimp boats wink in the bay, and the sound of a guitar, played very softly, caresses the ear in a tuneful whisper.

We are glad there are so few of us, and we hope Mulege will never become a fashionable place to visit. We want it for ourselves, and we promise not to tell. But I never could keep a secret.

He Wasn't a Gamefish

NAPLES, Fla.—It was a melancholy day. A chill wind from the northeast leaned against the windows of the weathered old structure on Marco Island where fishermen were conspiring a daybreak assault against tarpon.

Nothing quite approaches the dour mood of a summer resort on a stormy day. We peered gloomily through the windows as the wind and rain arrived in gusts under a sullen sky, whipping the laundry that had been hung on a clothesline from a fishing shack nearby.

A thin red-haired woman crouched between two automobiles, cupping her hands against the breeze in a futile effort to light a cigarette. A scrawny mongrel dog pawed at the screen door of the lodge, demanding entry. Inside, a sleepy-looking woman, hair askew, padded about the hallway in bathrobe and slippers. Grumpy fishermen peered into the kitchen, vainly sniffing for the aroma of perking coffee.

The fishermen had plotted and schemed against tarpon far into the night, but now they were defeated. Like Sonny Liston, they surrendered in the corner. The storm warnings were up and even the cormorants and pelicans were grounded. The fishermen eyed each other bleakly and brooded.

This was to have been the second day of the tournament, and the journalist types in the group had been framing the lead paragraphs of their dispatches. It was decided they should be written in the quaint style of the outdoor magazines.

Red Smith, the syndicated columnist, rehearsed us on the proper technique: "Get up!" cried Old Doc, "you'll never catch Old Squaretail lying in the sack."

We agreed to be up at dawn and nobody offered a word of protest when our guide, the estimable John Wilhelm of the Florida Development Commission, came clattering into our boudoir at a grisly hour. Wilhelm is an exceptional guide in every respect.

He is not only dependable with a wakeup call, but provides room service. The kitchen was closed downstairs but John served us steaming coffee from a thermos he had filled the previous evening.

"Gentlemen," Wilhelm announced cheerily, "today we are going to give the tarpon pluperfect hell."

Then he disappeared for a while, perhaps to wet a finger to the wind. He returned with grim news.

"No matter what Old Doc might say, we don't catch Mr. Squaretail today," said Wilhelm, "not in a high wind. You might as well get back in the sack."

Thus we were denied a rematch. We were as morose as the tourists in their $100 suites in Miami Beach, glowering at the deserted beaches. Florida isn't a pleasant place when they post frost warnings in late March, and somehow it didn't help when a voice on the radio assured us the weather was worse elsewhere.

The radio said it was 29 in New York and even colder in International Falls, but neglected to mention California. Oh, well. The tarpon will be waiting for us another day unless the real estate developers on Marco Island drain the swamp in the guise of progress. That would be a pity.

Fishing for baby tarpon (five to 20 pounds) among the Mangroves at Marco Island is truly a memorable experience. Nobody in our group boated one of the beasts but the contest, however one-sided, was exhilarating.

I had one strike and caught nothing but a slightly worn cowboy. With a clumsy backcast from a canoe, I succeeded in embedding the barbs of a plug in the skull of the senior pilot of Confidence Airlines, Mr. Colin Lofting, also known as Skipper.

Happily, Skipper lost neither his scalp nor his cool. He waited stoically for Wilhelm to arrive in the other canoe and perform surgery. Meanwhile, Skipper handed me his rod and commanded, "Keep casting!"

This was the first time I ever landed a pilot, instead of vice versa.

Lofting wore that red plug in his gray hair as though it were a decoration. Finally, Wilhelm, an old hand at this sort of thing, examined the victim.

"Skipper," he said, "this is going to hurt like the devil!"

Then he gave the plug a little twist and it came free. Skipper is a rugged hombre. He didn't yell or flinch. He didn't even rub the wound.

"Some of you newspaper types will do almost anything for column material," he said dryly.

Smith was great with sympathy. "Skipper," he said,
"you're not much of a gamefish. You only leaped
once."

For a blissful time the typewriter had been as quiet as
the stillness of a summer night in Montana. The old mill
gathered dust in a corner of our log cabin while I tempted
the brook trout with a mosquito fly in a gurgling stream
which followed an erratic course among the fir trees.

This is one definition of rapture. Since boyhood I had
longed to own a piece of ground in the mountains and we
had found it in western Montana—complete with a stand
of Christmas trees, a chuckling brook, a high, clear sky
beyond the reach of city lights, and solitude.

It's not very stylish, our little log cabin, and the
plumbing fixtures are vintage Chief Joseph. Of course,
we have running water—we run to the creek and run
back. But the water is pure because only fish bathe in it
and the trees are musical with a choir of birds.

Pollution is a camp fire. Noise is the sound of a truck
drumming its tires on the rutted road which serves our
cabin and four resident families. The serenity is such that
a passing car is a novelty. I'd walk to the porch and
wave and the man in the car would toot his horn in
acknowledgement.

We got acquainted with our neighbors quickly because

they are friendly and trusting. There remains a charming innocence among the folk in rural Montana, but manners conceal a core of realism.

"Do a man a bad turn around here," counseled one of our callers, "and you'll be lucky to get a sip of water out of Flathead Lake."

It's nice. There is a memory of the evening when we were sitting on the porch, glassing the meadows for whitetail deer, when a man and a small boy rode up on a horse and a pony, dismounted, and leaned against the rail fence.

We introduced ourselves and the man said, "Could I trouble you for some tobacco?"

I apologized. "Sure. But all I've got is pipe tobacco."

"That's what I meant," he said. Then he withdrew some thin paper from a shirt pocket, sprinkled it with tobacco, and rolled a cigarette. I hadn't seen that since I was a boy in rompers tagging at the heels of my grandfather.

It's been a moist summer in Montana and the first time we took the road to our cabin I was of a mood to sell the mortgage to the first man who asked. We slithered for nearly a mile in the slush while I battled the wheel and tried to avoid the ditches. Then we were grounded on a high center.

We stood in a chill rain and gathering darkness and the charm of Montana, the Big Sky Country, was in the eye of other beholders.

I found a shovel in a bulldozer left along the road by a forestry crew and attempted to dislodge our station wagon from the rocks and gumbo clay. I'd dig a while, then start the motor again. Nothing. We didn't advance a millimeter.

"Don't knock my country," one of the locals had told me earlier when I grumped about the rain. Sure. But at that moment Montana was the Big Drip Country.

"The way I feel right now," said my wife, "it's the Big Cry Country."

That sort of thing passes for humor when a car is in mud up to the axles on a lonely mountain road. But it gets better when help arrives.

This came in the form of three young men in a pickup truck who had gone bear hunting but instead found a pair of forlorn, muddy dudes.

The one at the wheel had a pleasant smile. "You folks picked an interesting place to park," he said by way of greeting.

They quickly effected a rescue, then shouted encouragement as we fishtailed in the slop until we reached firmer ground. We hurried to the shelter of the cabin which had been described as so snug "you can sit out the winter with a candle."

It's a nice little cabin, all right. But two candles stuck in empty wine bottles didn't warm it when the temperature dropped to 40 degrees and lower at sundown. We had more atmosphere than heat, and came to regard our down sleeping bags with affection.

We shared the place with Abe of Spoon River, a black Labrador who snores in a baritone voice, and a couple of pack rats who had homesteaded throughout the winter. The rats, Elmo and Edgar, played volleyball in the sleeping loft and merrily chased up and down the stairs until Elmo committed an indiscretion. He swiped my wife's silver cigarette lighter and left behind a pebble, his idea of a fair exchange.

Elmo died of a slight case of rat poison.

There Are Bears on Wild Bill

We were just getting settled into our little cabin in western Montana when a neighbor came to call and instructed us on the wild creatures in the area.

"Five bears," he said in a chatty tone, "have been killed off that front porch."

That got my wife's attention. She doesn't think bears

are cute or lovable. She even walks faster when she nears the bear exhibit at the zoo.

"If you ever meet a bear," the neighbor counseled, "the worst thing you can do is show fright. Don't shout. Don't run. Just stand there. The bear will go away."

This procedure didn't greatly appeal to my wife. "If I ever meet a bear, the problem will be resolved," she said. "I'll die on the spot."

Fortunately, this theory wasn't tested. Several two-legged critters stopped by for coffee and other refreshments, but the bears were wonderfully unsociable. There were reports of a sow and two cubs nibbling the wild strawberries on Wild Bill, the hill behind our cabin, but they made no public appearances.

This contributed to our peace of mind. I have no quarrel with bears and my only weapon was a .22 rifle which served for target practice. Later I learned a previous owner of the place actually had killed bears from the porch, but he baited them with garbage.

If the bears nosed about while we slept, they quickly learned we had no handouts for furry moochers. Each day I sacked the trash and garbage and drove it to a bin at the edge of the highway some five miles distant.

My idea of excitement was to sit on the porch in the evening and watch the shadows work up the slopes of three forested peaks which frame our little valley—Badger, Wild Horse and Blacktail. Once, while fly fishing on the little stream, I flushed a covey of ruffled grouse, a hen and her brood of chicks rising swiftly as the evening light played on their wings.

The cabin was totally bare when we took possession so we acquired the minimum creature comforts—a redwood table with two benches, and an old Frigidaire with a broken handle. The fridge cost $20 after I haggled a while with the salesman at the mercantile store.

First, he showed me a fancy one, a bargain at $175. I asked to see something less grand. Gradually, we went through the store, the price dropping, and then he led me to the warehouse. Reluctantly, he showed me the $20 beauty.

"That's what I had in mind," I told him.

He grinned. "I stalled as long as I could," he said.

The old fridge worked fine. It was so cold it froze everything, including the milk. And the steaks.

But we had lots of time for things to thaw. One night I gathered some small pine cones and brittle twigs to start the charcoal burning and then I grilled the steaks and we dined at the redwood table with candlelight and wild roses for atmosphere. I glanced out the picture window and a movement caught my eye.

"Look," I said, "we've got a visitor."

A small white-tailed buck was taking his evening meal from a bush about 20 yards from the cabin, down toward the creek. It was his swishing tail which attracted my attention. Fascinated, we watched silently, still.

Then I reached for my field glasses and the little buck saw the movement through the window. He bounded into the trees, his red coat glinting in the fading sun. In our lives, that will be remembered as a perfect moment.

Maybe that's why I felt a twinge of surprise a day or so later when a couple from up the valley appeared with their two handsome, scrubbed children to inspect the dudes in their midst.

"Why," said the lady, "you're just camping here."

We were, at that. Our beds were cots with sleeping bags and the light came from a single bulb connected to an extension cord and hung over a coat hook in the ceiling. Plus two Coleman lanterns. I thought it was chic. It was ours and it was cozy. The fish we ate for breakfast came from our creek.

It must have seemed different to others. One of our callers was a grizzled old fellow who lived about three miles away in a fine log house with three bedrooms. He heated it with an ingenious stove constructed of a 50-gallon barrel. He looked us over, and then decided he should tell my wife about the auction in town every Thursday night.

"You might want to buy a bedroom suite," he said gently.

BONDURAN, Ireland—It was an Irishman who observed that when God made time, he made plenty of it.

And that attitude has a direct bearing on why we were singing Irish songs with two new friends named Tom and Brian long past the witching hour of our second night in the Emerald Isle.

Our game plan was to catch fish in Lough Melvin, a substantial body of water in County Leitrim on the border that separates Ulster from the Irish Republic. We were assured the salmon and trout were so abundant they would leap into a man's hand unless he kept his fist tightly clenched.

But first came the singing. Ireland is a very musical place, a country full of laughter and song. Somehow we had gotten into the company of a pair of young officers from the Army of the Irish Republic and the bar was closing at the hotel and we were pleased to accept when they invited us to their quarters at the base.

Drinking and singing go together quite a bit in Ireland, and it is a blessing if one requires little in the way of sleep. Other friends came in as the night wore along and they sang sweetly and happily and ever so often Brian would leap from his chair and dance a jig or toss more peat on the fire and go for more whisky.

Occasionally I would glance at my watch and Brian would clap me on the shoulder and say, "Of course, you'll be having another?" It wasn't really a question, it was a command.

As I recall, there were maybe 10 of us in the living room of the bachelors' officers' quarters at that little army base near Bonduran, a resort community overlooking Donegual Bay, and we weren't very concerned about an invasion from the north.

"Do you have any idea when this party will end?" I asked Brian.

"Oh," he said cheerfully, "sometime around the middle of next month."

Now I understand why they say a man can never be lonely very long in Ireland. They are a wonderfully hospitable people, the Irish, and I hope I survive this visit.

I am prepared to believe anything about the Irish, even the stories Tom was telling about a space ship. It seems that a great ship was seen in the sky at a fair in County Sligo, and a spear was thrown from it and a man swam down through the clouds to retrieve it.

But there was a problem. Some in the crowd watching below had seized the spear and they held it until the visitor from space shouted that he was drowning. Considerately, they released the spear and he floated back to the space ship and climbed aboard. Then the vessel disappeared into the sky.

Hearing this story, I glanced again at my watch and noted that the hour was four o'clock of an April morning. I wondered if Brian would release the spear so I could sleep a while before going to Lough Melvin to contest the salmon and trout.

By now the whisky was gone, but Brian was undaunted. He went to the fridge and returned with a glass of dark ale.

"You have plenty of time," he assured me, "it won't be light for another hour."

At this season there is light in the Irish sky until 9 at night. When summer arrives, a man can stay on the lake with a flyrod until almost midnight or tee off at 9 p.m. and play 18 holes of golf before darkness catches him.

Our little party finally ran down when the ale, if not the Irish, was exhausted. An hour later reveille would be sounded but Tom and Brian no doubt would be very crisp and efficient in dealing with the troops. When I last saw them they were standing arm in arm on the porch of their little house, singing a song we had heard often during the night, a ditty that begins "I'm a poor, poor farmer..."

The singing, it developed, was superior to the fishing. Lough Melvin is a scenic place and it has a fine reputation among Irish anglers. It is a lake 7½ miles long and 1½ miles wide, a lake where De Cuellar, a captain in the Spanish armada, is said to have taken refuge after being wrecked on the Sligo coast.

Naturally, we arrived at the wrong time. Our guide was an Irishman with a Barry Fitzgerald face and he told us of catching 19 trout the previous week. But we couldn't raise them this time, not with a wet fly, and after a while he suggested that perhaps we'd like to walk a bit and see the pheasants in the fields nearby and inspect the ruins of Kossclougher Castle.

Of course, I don't expect to catch fish every time. The day was soft and shiny, the gorse on the shore line blazed with yellow blooms and it was a fine thing for a man with red eyes and a throbbing head to sit quietly in the boat while the guide rowed us to the dock.

The Irish can do almost anything, even cure warts by rubbing them with the cut face of a potato that has been dipped in fresh rain water. But they couldn't connect me to the trout, and that was providential. Anything bigger than a fingerling would have been a mismatch.

In mid-vacation there had come an invitation to try the summer steelhead fishing in Washington where, I was to learn, there are 142 rivers and streams populated with rainbow trout which go to sea and take on the manners and customs of salmon.

Red Smith hooked me with his first cast. "The Weyerhaeuser people want to show us how they can improve fishing by cutting trees," jested Smith on the phone from his summer home at Martha's Vinyard. "Meet me in Seattle and bring your fishing sticks."

The choice was not difficult. I had been using up valuable loafing time digging holes for avocado trees and staining bookshelves. Smith's proposal was irresistible.

I explained to my wife that I had been summoned for a research project—something about environment and ecology—and she just grinned while I packed my fishing rods. Three afternoons later we were on the shore of Lake Hancock in the Cascades, eating Gerry Emerick's steaks, waiting for the evening rise.

Gerry is the retired postmaster of Snoqualmie Falls who 30 years ago wrote a letter to the Weyerhaeuser timber people asking permission to build a cabin on their property at Lake Hancock. When the request went unanswered, Gerry wrote a second letter. Again silence. So Gerry built the cabin anyway.

The mail caught up with Gerry Emerick 28 years later. Suddenly there came a letter from a Weyerhaeuser official, asking Gerry to present himself at corporate head-quarters.

"Oh, oh," said Gerry. "I wonder if I should hire a lawyer and claim squatters' rights."

But Weyerhaeuser, it seems, has a corporate soul. When Gerry surrendered unarmed, he was invited to sign a land use permit. "You're welcome as long as you care to stay," said a vice president, amiably. "Just don't cut down any trees without asking permission."

Thus Gerry is not only friendly to Weyerhaeuser folk but cordial to newspaper types who arrive in quest of trout. Not long after we came across the lake with the help of a pair of outboard motors, Gerry was preparing a feast.

Mike Eads, purchasing agent at the Snoqualmie Falls mill, grilled rib steaks over charcoal and Gerry handled everything else. It was a meal fit for a hungry logger: fresh corn on the cob, a garden salad, potatoes, steak and apple pies just out of the oven.

"Take your time," urged Gerry, "there's no chance to catch fish while the sun is on the water."

Daylight saving is a blessing to the angler in the Pacific Northwest. We fished the last two hours of a splendid July afternoon, finally quitting at 10 o'clock. But no trout were killed, and the wounded were few in number.

Gerry caught a pair, one a brookie, the other a rainbow, trolling a fly. He put them back into the water quickly, entreating them to feed and grow. Smith gave us a fine display of his fly casting skill, but the fish were unimpressed. I fumbled with a fly rod for a while, then switched to a spinning outfit with a liquid bubble and a fly. Nothing.

"Sorry about the fishing," said Gerry, "but we've got coffee and pie at the cabin."

Some ate pie, others sipped of strong spirits. It was a cheerful time at the edge of the lake in Gerry's cabin among the towering Douglas firs. Gerry sat before his old upright piano and made lively, toe-tapping music.

We applauded his performance. "Not bad, I guess, for a $5 piano," said the artist.

Time passed swiftly and the hour was midnight when we again crossed the lake, this time using flashlights to find the place where the cars were parked. It was 2 a.m. when we groggily tumbled into our beds at a Tacoma motel.

"Get a good night's sleep," said Norm Nelson, "I'll be back to collect you at 6:30."

If you share the company of Norm Nelson, you learn to do without sleep. He's in public affairs for Weyerhaeuser and that means he goes fishing with journalists and mixes a bit of propaganda into the conversation. He speaks not of clear cutting, but of high yield forestry.

At breakfast on the second morning. Norm presented his game plan. We would be transported by helicopter to a high mountain lake in the Cascades for more trout fishing. On the third and fourth days we would get around to our primary mission: fishing for summer run steelhead.

We flew to Moolock Lake, altitude 3,908, in a 15-passenger helicopter deftly piloted by an old pro, Rod Kvamme. It was spectacular above the forested mountains of the Cascades; as Smith noted, there was never a time when we couldn't see at least three lakes.

He made this observation after Kvamme delicately placed the big bird in the only clear area along the shore of Moolock Lake. The noise of the helicopter had discouraged conversation and we wore ear muffs to screen the racket.

While we assembled our fishing gear, Kvamme roared away in the helicopter to plant fish for the Washington Game Dept. Presently he returned with a large orange bucket dangling beneath the copter. It contained 400 gallons of water and 4,000 trout fry. The helicopter hovered over the lake at an altitude of about 20 feet, the bottom of the bucket opened, and the fry spilled into the water and began a new life in Moolock Lake.

A game department biologist, Jim DeShazo, watched approvingly.

"Until the helicopter came along," said DeShazo, "we planted lakes with fixed wing aircraft and beaver ponds by back-packing. A back packer carries a pound of fry in five-gallon can. That's my idea of hard work."

Everybody Likes Stewfish

ANDROS ISLAND, Bahamas—Once it was the home base of Sir Henry Morgan, pirate, and now it is a favorite playground of those who regard combat with bonefish as a sporting proposition.

We had come to the northern shore of Andros Island—the largest of the 700 islands in the Bahamas—after hearing the sand flats were matted with bonefish. Incredibly, this was true. Or what passes for truth among fishermen.

We did see hundreds, or perhaps thousands, of the sleek, silver bullets swimming in schools in the shallow waters around Rum Key and Cattle Key. We tempted them with crabs and we even caught a few bones and brought them to the big net carried by our Bahamian guide, Mosser Evans.

Mosser Evans is a man I will remember. I would never have caught a bone without Mosser. Indeed, I wouldn't even have seen a bone.

Mosser not only found the bonefish but he taught me how to walk in bonefish water.

"Walk light," he instructed, "walk soft, walk cool."

Mosser had carried us to the bonefish country in an air boat designed to run over a teaspoon of water or, if necessary, wet grass. The air boat travels at high speed and gives off a volume of noise several decibels louder than a lovelorn moose. We might have been deafened by the sound but Mosser thoughtfully provided rubber ear-muffs.

Or, like Mosser, we might have adjusted to the roar of the engine. Nothing bothers Mosser. At the end of the day, I had such a nasty sunburn on my legs and feet I was able to walk only with greatest difficulty. Mosser was dancing the limbo while a calypso band made joyful sounds in the bar at the Andros Beach Hotel.

Mainly, though, I admire Mosser because he taught us to stalk bonefish. He could see them very plainly when I could see only water, sand and grass. I had assumed we would chase the bones in the air boat but the boat spooks the bones and Mosser dropped the anchor and we got out and walked.

We waded in warm, clear water which splashed above our ankles. We followed Mosser, trying to walk light and cool, while he searched for schools of bones. The attitude of his body told me when a bone had caught his eye.

Mosser is a tall, skinny man, very black, and on this day he wore a faded baseball cap that once had been dark blue, an old Army shirt with PFC chevrons on each sleeve, and yellow swim trunks. He carried a big net under his left arm, cupped the bait in his left hand, and held a fishing rod in his right hand.

When the bones were near, Mosser would lean forward like a birddog on a point and aim his rod at the fish. He would walk very quietly, his feet coming out of the water with each step, and then he would fling the sea crab before the school of bones with a sidearm delivery.

The first requirement of bonefishing is to see the fish against an indistinct, beige background. The rest of the art is casting against the trade winds that blow endlessly through the islands of the Bahamas chain. I would cast and the wind would return the bait to my feet like a boomerang.

"Cast sidearm, mon," counseled Mosser. He's the Don Drysdale of Bahamian guides.

With patience and determination, we finally learned something of the technique and soon Red Smith, the poet laureate of New Caanan, Conn., was battling a bone. Smith accurately describes bones as the sprinters among fish; they go very strongly for six furlongs, then tire. This one made three big runs before he brought it to Mosser's net.

"Do we keep it or release it?" asked the triumphant angler.

The question surprised Mosser. "Everybody likes stew-fish and potato bread on Sunday," came the reply. "Tomorrow is Sunday."

After a while, Smith caught another bone; the fish took off with a whoosh, made a big run and then came to the net as though it had trained for a three-round fight. I wouldn't say that Smith was gloating but he looked awfully pleased with himself.

Later in the day, when we were sitting at the outdoor bar with the thatched roof beside the beach, the other hotel guests would politely inquire about the fishing and Smith was always the first to respond.

"Modesty forbids me to mention who caught the most fish," he would begin. The word smug was created expressly to describe a certain type of fisherman.

Actually, Smith is a gracious gentleman who does not regard fishing as a competitive sport and he exhorted Mosser to connect me with a bone. And the guide, a truly remarkable man, did just that.

A bone took my bait, I held him while he made two, long swift runs, and brought him to the net. I had avoided being skunked by the elite of gamefish and I was glowing when the air boat brought us back to Lowe's Sound after a 45-minute ride over choppy water. Then we rode in an old station wagon to the hotel where a sign at the door invited, "Have A Hobie Day."

We did.

Get Mother Out of the Tree

We were circling over the Meling Ranch in Baja California, trying to establish if we had the right address, when the pilot noted something on the dirt runway.

"I hope this isn't an omen," said Carl Molling as he pointed the Aero Commander toward earth, "but there's a buzzard waiting at the end of the landing strip."

It wasn't. Molling sat the little craft down smoothly and the buzzard, feeling cheated, flew off to scout for new prospects while we unloaded our luggage and guns into a pickup truck which materialized quite suddenly. A Mexican cowboy delivered us to Ada Meling, one of the great and famous ladies of Lower California, and thus began a four-day idyll at Rancho San Jose.

I had voiced an ambition to shoot some quail and, with luck, to meet Ada's pioneering parents, Salvi and Alberta Meling, and her brother, Andrew, who once rode a mule 1,300 miles the length of Baja California, a trip that required six months and a day. When I finally saw Andrew, I wasn't surprised that his legs form a parenthesis.

The Melings are interesting people. Alberta Meling, the dowager queen of the peninsula, soon will observe her 82nd birthday and a heart condition has restricted her activities somewhat. I couldn't see her right away because she was climbing an apple tree.

This attracted the attention of a family friend from Long Beach, Dr. Ralph Young.

"You'd better get your mother out of that tree," the physician protested to Ada.

"No, you tell her," came the reply, "she might listen to you."

Physicians who visit the Meling Ranch become accustomed to strange requests. One night they called upon the doctor to supervise the arrival of 10 tiny brown pups. Tinker Bell, the Meling collie, had appropriated one of the family bedrooms as a maternity ward and the father, a handsome but ill-tempered Belgian shepherd named Fox, stood before the door making sounds deep in his throat.

Now, however, the physician went off to reason with the lady in the tree. He was laughing when he returned.

"She won't come down," he reported. "Says she's not really climbing—she has one foot on a ladder."

The Melings have been part of the lore and legend of Baja California since 1908, and the guest ranch supervised by Ada is celebrated as a warm and hospitable place. Ada is of Norwegian, Danish and English extraction, and she is that rare woman who blends masculine efficiency with feminine charm.

"I'm Mexican," she says, "as apple pie."

She makes a fine apple pie from Mexican apples, and sets a spendid table. The dining room in the evening makes a nice scene. A fire blazing in the old Franklin stove, the soft glow of kerosene lamps, and the long table crowded with happy wing shooters.

Friends from neighboring ranches are apt to appear at any hour. This can lead to guitar playing and singing and great contentment. The guests may leave very suddenly or, on the other hand, they may not go home at all. On certain nights one can arise at three in the morning and join an excellent party.

Much of Baja California looks as though it had been created when God was in bad humor. But the Meling Ranch has that most precious of all virtues: water. It is green and lovely and tree-shaded and at this time of year there is a crispness in the air hinting of autumn.

The ranch nestles in a valley, about 200 miles south of San Diego, 50 miles inland from the Pacific, at an altitude of 2,200 feet. I went there on the advice of counselor. Which is to say that two attorney friends, Howard Turrentine and Tom Hamilton, recommended we assemble there with our wives to seek quail and recreation.

We saw thousands of quail and a rather substantial

number even fell into our clutches. Turrentine must be an extraordinary marksman; twice he scored Scotch doubles—meaning he dropped two birds with one shot. Then, happily, in the evening we had a number of double scotches while relaxing before the hearth.

They were needed. Once Turrentine opened the cooler where the birds were stored until they could be cleaned and a quail flew out. But Howard's Labrador, Lupe, retrieved it a second time.

We had superb wine from Hamilton's cellar, and the finest company, and the shooting was exceptional. It was the first time I ever willingly broke my shotgun and packed it in the case. On the last day my wife and I took a long hike, leaving the guns behind, and we watched, fascinated, while a road runner stalked a large covey of quail. Always they stayed just beyond the reach of the enemy.

Next time, with equal luck, we will shoot more birds and Andrew Meling and his wife, Cathy, have invited us to visit them in the San Pedro Martin mountains where, at the 9,200-foot level, they are involved with the construction of an observatory. This is wild and beautiful country, they say, where the wind blows in gales up to 40 miles per hour and the water already is freezing in mid-day. Andrew and Cathy are up there in sleeping bags.

He Lives With Bald Eagles

FLAMINGO, Fla.—A cloud of birds lifted suddenly from a spit of rock and sand as we sliced through the choppy surface of Florida Bay in John West's small, hand-crafted skiff.

"They're mostly gulls and willets," said West as the creatures circled and keened under a buttermilk sky, "but look hard and you can see the eagle's nest. You might see the female around. Too bad there's not enough water to take you closer; we've been getting great pictures."

I must admit I am a bit envious of John West. In retirement, he has an idyllic life. He is a birder, a man who fills his days by observing the gaudy wildlife of the Everglades National Park, a sanctuary for more than 300 species of birds. Some are common, some are rare, all are interesting.

Through the intercession of Dan Tomlinson, manager of the Flamingo Lodge, we had made an appointment with West to view the roseate spoonbill, the eagle, the osprey and other birds of the Everglades at their rookery on Frank Key. West makes a modest living (he's a retired border patrolman) identifying and explaining birds to tourists who can't distinguish between a buzzard and an eagle or a flamingo and a roseate spoonbill.

His manner is proprietary. "There are 50 pairs of bald eagles in the park," he explained, "I have five pair."

Association with birds evidently is good for one's disposition. West has much sun and happiness on his face and he stands tall and erect in his little skiff. It occurred to me that even the great white heron must envy his long legs.

Rain was threatening when we arrived at Frank Key in late afternoon. West shut off the outboard motor and we drifted close to a grove of Mangrove trees where the birds of the Everglades have established residence without being troubled by zoning laws and tax notices.

"There are more bird nests per territory here than any other island in the park," said West. He sniffed the wind like a birddog scenting a covey of quail. "You fellas are going to get wet, but don't worry. It won't be a drencher."

The birder of Flamingo isn't infallible. After a while the rain came in torrents and we got soaked. West chuckled as he reached for his foul weather gear.

"Did I say it wouldn't be a drencher?" he asked. His eyes twinkled behind his spectacles.

But, no matter. The rain held off until we had

observed the occupants of the Frank Key rookery with a sense of wonder and delight.

Roseate spoonbills festooned the Mangrove branches like red roses on a thorn bush. Migratory white pelicans, who come to Florida with other tourists in this season, were heaped like a snowbank on a sandbar. Brown pelicans fished in the shallow waters. An osprey soared overhead. A shy reddish egret passed a stick to a suitor partly obscured by the foliage.

The reddish egrets fascinated West. "See how they pass the stick back and forth," he said. "I think it's a mating ritual, but I'm not sure."

The reddish egret is a large bird with a gray body and a rusty neck and head. It is considered an endangered species because of the wanton ways of man; thousands of these lovely creatures were slaughtered by plume hunters in times past. But they are flourishing again in this sanctuary.

"Last night," said our guide, "there was a flight of 200 to 300 reddish egrets and that was exciting. They're supposed to be comparatively rare."

West directed our attention to a flock of crows perched in a Mangrove tree near a comorant nest where the chicks were screeching for their evening meal.

"The crows," he explained, "are hoping to steal eggs from the comorant's nest. If the comorants leave their nest unguarded even for a few seconds, they'll be filling out a burglary report. Earlier this week, I saw the crows hit a nest and get two eggs quick."

If the crows are robbers, the brown pelicans are beggars. Despite his awkward appearance, the bown pelican lands with the grace of a jumbo jet at the marina in Buttonwood Canal and there he waits for leftovers at the fish cleaning tables. He is the garbage disposal of the Everglades.

The white pelican is more dignified. He scoops up fish in shallow water when he comes to Florida to escape winter in Utah where he nests. This tourist begins arriving in October and goes home in April.

"You know when the white pelican is getting ready to leave," said West. "For two or three days you see the birds searching for an updraft that will take them north, then suddenly they're gone. I suppose you know they are the heaviest-bodied bird that soars."

I was especially taken with the roseate spoonbill, described by park biologist William B. Robertson, Jr., as "the strangest and most unmistakable" of the Everglade birds. The adults have bright pink wings with carmine epaulets, red legs, and an odd spoon-shaped beak. They fish in communal style, herding their prey into shallow water, and eat by swinging their bills from side to side.

It was a splendid day, even though it ended in a slashing rain. As any wet birder knows, a hot shower and a toddy is good for the body.

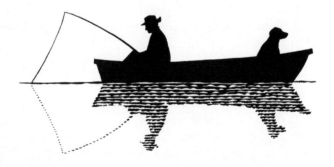

It seems a magical and mysterious place. Corrizo Gorge. Habitat of bighorn sheep, golden eagles, rattlesnakes, mourning dove, coyotes and quail. A repository of memories of the Chinese workmen who labored for 12 years to construct a rail link between El Centro and San Diego more than a half century ago.

In recent times the little grand canyon of San Diego County has been even more remote and inaccessible to the public than was the San Vizcaino Desert of Baja

California before a modern highway slithered the length of the peninsula. The San Diego and Arizona Eastern Railway discontinued passenger traffic through Corrizo Gorge in 1951 and subsequent efforts to establish scenic tours have aborted.

Now the silence of the gorge is disturbed only by the commotion of two freight trains which daily chug over the wooden trestles and through the cool tunnels on the rim of the world between Jacumba and Dos Cabezas.

I went there on a recent day in the company of game wardens Bob Jordan and Bill Powell as an observer while they searched this vast, raw and fascinating area for bighorn sheep and the major enemy of these splendid animals—man. Corrizo Gorge is forbidden terrain to all but railroad personnel and law enforcement types: border patrolmen, deputy sheriffs and game wardens.

The wardens justified my presence as a caddy or a trainee or something of the sort. Somewhat grumpily, Ben Wyly assented. Wyly is the supervisor for the section of the railroad which hangs on the lip of Corrizo Gorge and he is strict about trespassers.

Man is unwelcome in the gorge because his behavior is often destructive. He disturbs the precious sheep, he starts fires, he is malicious. At the foot of the gorge there is a lovely grove of palm trees which are just now regaining their health and beauty. They had been badly scorched by poachers who wantonly fired tracer bullets in the hope of igniting a fire. Regrettably, they succeeded.

The wardens are greatly concerned by the intrusion of four-wheeled vehicles which violate the sanctity of this refuge for bighorn sheep. The sheep are easily frightened and driven from their watering places.

Man is the sheep's most deadly foe, but not his only concern. The coyote and the mountain lion have the taste of a gourmet; they are partial to rack of lamb.

We came upon a young ram freshly killed by a coyote. It was a fascinating episode in nature. The coyote was eating lunch when he became aware of our presence.

Startled, he bolted and ran through the rocks and cactus.

His first thought was safety, his second thought came from his stomach. The coyote ran with a hindquarter of the young ram in his jaws.

Bill Powell drew a pistol, a .357 magnum, and fired a shot into the air. The gorge was filled with this hostile sound. He got the coyote's attention. The animal dropped the hind quarter and gathered speed until he was beyond the range of a gun. Then he stood and glowered at us.

"The biggest coyote I've ever seen," said Bob Jordan.

And the darkest. He had the look of a timber wolf.

Powell drew his knife and severed the head of the lamb from the ravaged remains of his torso. The coyote had eaten well, his belly was heavy. There were two nubbins of horns on the skull of the yearling lamb; one day he would have been a magnificent ram. The nubbins would never grow into curls.

Such is the design of nature. We had hoped to find evidence of the chukkar partridges released many years ago by the Department of Fish and Game. But Ben Wyly warned us the quest would be futile.

"Once," he said, "it was possible to see as many as 200 chukkars in the gorge but they're gone. Hunters got them."

He paused while the thought made us angry. "Not two-legged hunters. Golden eagles. For a while, our two eagles were well fed."

Wyly's knowledge of Corrizo Gorge is intimate. He's served the San Diego and Arizona Eastern Railway for 38 years; he's searched the barren construction camp sites for old coins; he knows every watering hole for the sheep in that stretch of the De Anza State Park; he's killed more rattlesnakes along the roadbed than he cares to remember.

Ben has a sense of humor. He took the rattles from several snakes and fitted them into a necklace, placing the male and female rattles in proper sequence.

Visitors to his home in Jacumba are impressed when he displays a string of 21 rattles.

"They ask how big the snake was," says Ben, chuckling. "I tell them, 'oh, maybe 18 feet.' "

If the gorge yielded an 18-foot rattler, I wouldn't be surprised. It is the residence of a 185-foot wooden railroad trestle, the world's highest. The bones in the canyon include derailed box cars ("the engineer went to sleep") which provided some mellow moments. The cargo: beer and wine.

"Some of the fellows weren't walking very steady coming out of the gorge," said Ben Wyly, dryly.

Cheers from the Calico Cat

In late afternoon I would bring the brook trout up from the creek which runs strongly in all seasons and the female calico cat would be waiting at the doorstep, purring in anticipation.

The place I go to kill fish is not one of the more celebrated streams of Montana. It's just a creek which flows through the timber of our piece of land in Flathead County, so undistinguished and obscure I have never met another angler along its grassy banks.

It is exactly right for me because the pools and the fast water are infested with lively, unsophisticated brook trout who can't resist a tuft of hair which conceals a barbed hook. And they are delightfully ferocious when tempted by a grasshopper or a worm.

Thus we had the pleasant aroma of frying trout rising from a skillet in our one-room log cabin and the calico cat, known as Bandit, scratched at the screen door, clamoring for admission. The calico and a sleek black tomcat belong to a young couple who rent our cabin in winter and most other seasons, and the creatures accepted us without prejudice.

Montana is a hospitable place. Stop a stranger along a mountain road to ask information about a good huckleberry patch and he'll likely insist you go home with him and get the answer over a cup of coffee. I have the impression that coffee is brewing at all hours throughout western Montana.

Montana is a place of great charm because it is unhurried. The pace is slow and slower. At least that's true around Kalispell. Kalispell is the seat of Flathead County and it was here that Evel Knievel hatched his idea of soaring over the Snake River Canyon in a jerry built rocket. Naturally, this inspiration seized him while he was in a saloon.

Evel's grandmother is a Kalispell celebrity in her own right. She makes wonderful huckleberry jam and preserves. Kalispell is a good place to eat. There's a restaurant on Main Street which features the best pastie this side of Wales. They call it the Butte pastie, an allusion to the Welsh miners who brought this tasty dish to Montana.

Kalispell, situated at the northern tip of vast Flathead Lake, is crowded in summer with campers and water skiers and fisherpersons and tourists en route to Glacier National Park. But it empties when frost brings autumn dress to the trees. The permanent population of Kalispell is 12,000, Flathead County has 40,000 residents, and the population of Montana still numbers less than a million.

It's a good place to unwind. I doubt there is much demand for shrinks in Montana. My idea of therapy is the solitude of a pretty creek where the only sounds are rushing water and wind in the trees.

I had success with the brookies because I have come to know where the wild trout lurk in this brook and a friend, Ed Hey, taught me about stealth and patience. The brookies are skittish and suspicious. Show yourself to them, make a noise, let your shadow fall on the water, and you'll depart with an empty creel.

"Approach with care," counseled Hey, "those brookies feel the vibrations of your feet."

The technique works. I felt a sense of accomplishment because I caught brookies where I expected to catch them. For years I've heard knowledgeable anglers talk about reading trout waters and this happy experience brought a glimmer of understanding. You see a brookie flashing in the pure stream, you set your hook, and you've got him.

A while later you come up from the creek and display the contents of your creel to your wife and the calico cat and the applause is sweet. The cat has good reason to flatter the mighty angler; she is well fed during our stay.

It pleased me to deliver a mess of the brookies to my fishing coach, Ed Hey. Ed is great with wisdom on all practical matters, but he's been on injured reserve since submitting to back surgery, a fusion, that didn't work very well. He is an artist, a carver, who fashions splendid belt buckles from the horn of moose and elk and he insisted that I accept one of his treasures, a bighorn sheep carving, as a gift.

I argued until Ed got a certain glint in his eye. This good man lives with such pain he is obliged to rest after 30 minutes of intense work, each carving represents 10 hours of hard labor. The pieces are a bargain at $100.

"I sell them to strangers," he said, gruffly, "I give them to friends. You are my friend."

A nice place, Montana.

Chapter 5

ABE THE LADIES' MAN

Give me the young man who has brains enough to make a fool of himself.

Robert Louis Stevenson

He won't discuss it, but I suspect my friend, Abe of Spoon River, has a romantic interest.

For the first four years of his life Abe has been too preoccupied with training for big matches to notice girls. I assume he still wants the world's retriever championship, but lately he has seemed less dedicated.

Actually, it all began when he found a hole in the fence at the foot of the canyon. Soon he was staying out after bedcheck and trying to sneak in while we were occupied with the late news. We weren't sure whether that was Sen Sen on his breath, or just the aroma of liquor.

Abe is clever but inexperienced. He even smuggled a couple of pillows under a blanket, trying to create the illusion of his presence. But the ruse was quickly exposed. The pillows didn't snore.

He blushed when I suggested the time had come for a

man-to-man talk about the birds and the bees. I mean, I think he blushed; Abe is a black Labrador Retriever and you don't always know when he's embarrassed.

All the boys at my house are very secretive. The teenaged heir locks himself in the basement rumpus room when he discusses affairs of state on the telephone. And Abe is the sort who wouldn't tell if they put lighted matches under his toenails.

The generation gap has come between us. For the first time since Abe moved in with us, there is a problem of communication. I've got a bride picked out for him, an Illinois lady of aristocratic lineage, but Abe thinks matchmaking is old-fashioned. I suspect he has been running around with Airedales and other low types.

I tell him he'll never be a champion with this attitude. Dames and training are as combustible as fire and gasoline. I talk to him the way Deacon Jack Hurley talks to his fighters. Women have ruined more good athletes than war and pestilence.

Abe listens politely, but he doesn't seem to hear. We turn him out in the yard in the evening and he disappears.

Now we have what is known as the fence crisis. If Abe is to be shielded from scheming females, not to mention careless motorists and conniving dogcatchers, we'll have to replace the old fence around the yard.

We have been getting estimates from fencing companies and an undertone of tension is creeping into the family councils. The keeper of the budget is appalled by the high price of romance. She observes that the money we propose to spend on that fence would also purchase such frills as rugs, lamps and slip covers and, really, the house could be a very attractive place.

The effect of all this is traumatic. My sleep is disturbed and I find my behavior has become eccentric. It's very distracting to see Abe lying innocently at my feet, watching me with one eye, and know he's planning to go over the wall at the first opportunity.

The other evening I was dressing for a formal dinner

and trying to observe Abe from the bedroom window at the same time. If he bolted for the fence, I intended to call him back with an authoritative shout. As I watched, Abe checked the gate and strolled away.

When he disappeared from view, I became very nervous. I always have trouble with a bow tie and shirt studs and now, trying to hurry, dressing seemed incredibly complicated. Later in the evening I discovered I had jumped into a pair of black slacks instead of tuxedo trousers. The socks didn't match, either.

Abe's display of independence has undermined my posture as a strict disciplinarian. He's always been so cooperative, so humble, so eager to please. Now, he would rather run around with girls who drink and smoke and wear bright nail polish than chase a training dummy.

My wife, a perceptive lady, has decided Abe has merely been humoring me all this time. He still won't enter or leave a room until I give him a signal but this, she is convinced, is merely youth patronizing the whims of an old man. He has a stubborn streak as wide as a river and the patience to bend me to his will. When my back is turned, he goes over the fence.

Sure, the poets rhapsodize about spring and young love and blooming flowers and all that jazz. It's wonderful, I suppose. But it means a new fence.

When Abe of Spoon River came to us as a pup of six months, his first challenge was to establish rapport with the vice president in charge of flower beds.

He had been preceded by a large, sturdy poodle — the kind French farmers harness to carts — who amused himself by chewing holes in the garden hoses and digging up geranium plants. We called him Pepe Lamoca, Jr., but I'm not going to tell you how my wife addressed him because her comments were off the record. Colorful, too.

That made it harder for Abe. He was guilty until proved innocent. As I recall, it took about 24 hours to clear his name.

Nobody, not even the vice president in charge of tidy housekeeping, can resist a beautiful Labrador Retriever when he places his head in your lap and looks at you with eyes brimming with love.

Now Abe has been with us four years, and the way he charmed that woman is a scandal. She doesn't even protest when he sprawls on her precious Oriental rug.

The big thing about Abe is his couth. He is a gentleman of refinement, his manners are elegant. Unusually.

He will enter the living room in a state of high excitement and sometimes he sends the Oriental rug flying against the fireplace screen. But he quickly recovers his composure. Then, one by one, he pays his respects to each member of the family.

Not being a continental type, I've never been much for hand kissing. But that's very much Abe's style. He sure knows how to get along with the ladies.

Abe is the soul of courtesy. He never enters or leaves a room without requesting permission. Leaving, he pauses before each member of the family, awaiting a signal or an indication. I suspect he would sit before an open door for three days.

During dinner he becomes a shadow against the dining room wall. Not a sound, not even a sigh, passes his lips. Then I push back my chair and he materializes instantly. Abe comes with the coffee and cognac.

This is the time when he is especially loving and attentive to the missus. She strokes his black head, scratches his chin and rubs his ears. He is faint with love.

Part of Abe's charm is his quiet, unobtrusive manner. He never ties up the telephone, turns up the volume on the TV set, or interrupts a conversation. And he is solid and responsible.

When I'm gone overnight, he sleeps just inside the front door. When I'm home, he sleeps at the top of the staircase.

His hearing is remarkable. The missus can sit in the living room and watch Abe's reactions on the patio and know whether friend or stranger is approaching. His tail tells the tale. If the tail is busy, he's preparing a warm welcome. If he stands quietly at the gate, tail motionless, it is the occasion to be wary.

But he is peaceful by nature. He has even reached an accord with the skunks who share his playground. There are indications they have been drinking from his water pan, but Abe doesn't make an issue of it. He is a gentleman; gentlemen don't drink with skunks. His dignity is intact.

Abe is circumspect, and he is sly. It is the missus' custom to send him outdoors when the boss leaves for work. Knowing this, Abe tends to become inconspicuous.

Sometimes she finds him curled up on the elk rug in the den. When he gets to his feet, a study of innocence, he makes a strange appearance. The elk rug sheds, you see, and Abe seems to sprout a set of gray whiskers.

More often he tries to avoid notice by sleeping at the head of the stairway. Out of sight, out of mind, he figures.

Abe isn't perfect. Once he tried to retrieve a live mockingbird and turned over the bird bath. More recently he left his footprints in the missus' new flower bed. Once a week a lady comes in to clean the place and, for a few hours, Abe gets no response when he scratches at the door.

Without considering the gravity of the crime, I admit him. This provokes a strong protest about careless husbands who make dirt and work, and I slink away, using the excuse that I have forgotten to buy wine or tobacco or Creole pralines.

When I return a few minutes later Abe is snug on the frayed Oriental rug, snug and smug. I find this somewhat confusing, not to say inconsistent and contradictory, and demand an explanation.

"Well," says the missus, "he looked cold and unhappy on the patio and, besides, I can't keep the house immaculate anyway."

Did you ever see a Labrador grin?

I really should save this item for Eileen Jackson because it's one of the major social events of the season. What I'm trying to say is that Mr. and Mrs. Jack Murphy announce the betrothal of Abe of Spoon River and Lady B Good.

Miss B Good recently arrived from her home in Crystal Lake, Ill., and will celebrate Christmas with friends and family of her fiancee. A series of parties are planned for the popular young couple, and the nuptials are tentatively scheduled in January. Leftovers will be served.

This merger between two prominent families of Labrador Retrievers means Abe, as he is known to close friends, will have to yield his membership in the bachelor's club.

Abe and Lady were introduced at Lindbergh Field

when she arrived for the holidays. This romance wasn't made in heaven, it was arranged by a professional matchmaker. Abe's fiancee was sent to him by Mr. Jay G. Odell from the Consort Kennels in Crystal Lake. All the ladies at Consort are debutantes and Lady has such distinguished forbears she's doubtless a contessa at the very least.

Abe flipped when he met Lady. Actually, I thought he was a bit forward. I mean these are very speedy times and all that, but Abe was nuzzling this chick in a display of affection some might consider embarrassing. He was struck by the thunderbolt. Abe melted.

In time Abe will learn about the society of the females. He'll learn they can be explosive the first time he tries to drop one. But now he's enchanted. Until Lady arrived, Abe thought wing shooting was about the best thing this tired old world has to offer.

I wouldn't be surprised if he starts growing a mousstache and bathing regularly. Not that personal hygiene isn't a good thing. If Lady can persuade Abe to stop shedding black hair all over the house, she'll be more valuable than a vacuum cleaner.

But Abe is a strong character and I don't think he'll be henpecked. For years the mistress of the house has been arguing with Abe because he takes his afternoon nap in the flower bed beside the patio. He isn't very welcome in the flower bed and he aggravates the situation by digging a hole to make himself comfortable.

This provokes exclamations of protest, and sometimes the words are harsh. Abe is very contrite and he lowers his head and slinks away. Then, when the tumult quiets, he sneaks back to the flower bed and starts kicking dirt on the patio again.

Abe has been described as stubborn, and I hope Lady doesn't think she's going to reform him. As a bachelor of six years, his habits are pretty well set. Still, all the girls agree he's quite a catch.

I'll bet Lady's heart would have been thumping if she

could have watched Abe working chukkar and pheasant at Bud Pepper's gun club near Ramona a few days ago. We took just one leisurely sweep through the field, and Abe and his high-spirited half brother, Rip, found and retrieved all the birds planted by Pepper.

This is known as artificial or put-and-take hunting but it seemed real to the men and the dogs. The terrain at Pepper's ranch is just about perfect for bird shooting and this was one of Abe's best days. He worked close to the guns, flushing the birds within range. But he lost many of the retrieves to Rip, who is quicker and more aggressive. That seemed fair enough because Rip's master, Bob, shot most of the game.

We returned with a mixed bag of chukkar, pheasant, persimmons and mistletoe. We always enjoy shooting with Bud because he's agreeable company and his 1,800-acre ranch provides excellent cover for the planted birds. A secondary attraction is the delicious water from his well. I'd make the trip just to watch Bob's companion, Rip, drink from the faucet. Of course, that's a bit primitive for Abe. He laps his water from a pan.

Now, on Christmas Day, Abe lies on the rug just inside the front door and dreams of his true love, Lady B Good. Each time I pass he raises his head inquiringly and often he shows affection by thrusting his nose against my hand. I like seeing him there. He fits.

It's nice to walk into a room during the holidays and see a Christmas tree aglow and the fire leaping in the fireplace where Santa descended last night with gifts for my grandson, Chris, though Chris was pretty sure the chimney was too small for Santa and suggested it might be a good idea to leave a window open or a door ajar.

Still, it must have gone well. No sound was heard during the night and there was a fire truck and a football helmet and some other interesting things under the tree for Chris, and Abe, hearing the visitor, just thumped his tail. Nobody with a heart full of love is going to bark at Santa.

Life With Father

Since the pups were whelped, we have taken to addressing the sire as Frazier, the Labrador.

Abe of Spoon River, who is getting along in years is the father of a splendid brood of eight. Seven males and a female. In the beginning there were 10, but two males were lost at birth despite tender care by the mother, Ms Tara.

A beautiful girl, Ms Tara. A mate worthy of the magnificent Abe.

Tara is a society lady from the Consort Kennel of Crystal Lake, Ill. Even the Astors and the Vanderbilts would be impressed by her breeding.

Until Abe met Tara, he intended to remain a bachelor. He had carried on a flirtation with a flighty thing named Lady B Good, but the chemistry was wrong.

We had begun to fret about whether Abe would produce an heir. He'll be nine years old in June and his whiskers are gray, he's lost a step or two.

But, like Frazier the lion, he was just biding his time.

When Abe decided to perpetuate himself, there was a population explosion.

Abe's prestige is very high. I've been passing out cigars and ordering champagne. And my wife has been trying to square herself with Fraz — beg pardon, Abe.

"Oh mighty Sire," I heard her tell Abe, "please forgive me for the unkind things I've said about you."

He accepted the lady's apology. He leaned against her, eager for a caress.

Yet he is not without conceit. I detect a bit of a strut in his walk. Any time now I expect to find him at the door with a carnation between his teeth. When I toss the training dummy he chases it eagerly and returns it without panting. I suspect he is holding his breath.

He is possessed of a strong sense of dignity. He does

not suffer fools gladly. When Heathcliff the cat competes for the training dummy, Abe pretends not to notice. But Heathcliff feels that withering glare and retreats discreetly.

Heathcliff is a black tomcat who moved in with us some months ago.

Once Abe was a skinny little fellow of six months, all legs, elbows and sharp angles. Now he is broad of girth and his skin is too tight.

Given a chance, he'll retrieve birds until he almost literally drops from fatigue. But age brings a degree of wisdom, even to Labradors. Abe has learned to pace himself. If there's a lull during a day of wing shooting, he finds a shady spot and snoozes. He conserves his strength.

He sleeps, eats and hunts. And runs around with high-bred girls. No wonder he has such a good disposition.

He has reason to be pleased with himself because his progeny are a handsome lot. I get the pick of the litter and the rest of the pups belong to my daughter. Naturally, two of Abe's issue have been named Isaac and Ishmael. It would be perfect if the mother were Sarah, instead of Tara.

But Tara is close enough. Tara, like Abe, comes to us from Crystal Lake, Ill. Which is to say she is a gift from my young friend, Jay G. Odell. Jay has been eligible for Social Security for more than two decades.

An amazing dog, Abe. Mr. Odell was ecstatic when we phoned him at his winter home in Venice, Fla., to announce the arrival of Isaac, Ishmael and six other infants.

"I couldn't be more proud of the old chap," he said, "buy him a steak on me."

Today a letter arrived from Venice and it ended with the exclamation "whoopee!"

Those are my sentiments precisely.

First came Abe of Spoon River. Then, naturally, followed Isaac, Son of Abraham.

Abe, at 9, is becoming rather senior for a Labrador Retriever and friends convinced us that the company of his son, Isaac, would be a tonic. The puppy, it was reasoned, would compel Abe to be more active and add years to his life.

The logic disarmed me. It was my recollection that puppies are mischievous, destructive and occasionally amusing. But I yielded to the argument that Abe is entitled to companionship, and the idea of the old boy grooming an heir had a certain appeal.

So much for fantasy.

Abe does not thank me for this kindness. He's too tired. He hasn't had a good night's rest since the puppy took up residence. That was the occasion when Ike awakened us with an eerie, grieving cry passed down from a distant ancestor. A banshee, perhaps. It was chilling.

We live in an old house which pops and creaks and, sometimes, with the approach of midnight when we are gathered in the living room, footsteps and other sounds can be heard in the attic. The thought of sharing the place with a ghost delights my wife and son, and I pretend not to notice.

"There's old Brandenburg shuffling about in his bedroom slippers," says my wife with a smile.

I can't explain Brandenburg. He's a secret shared by my wife and son. And Heathcliff, the cat.

It's my theory that Isaac, Son of Abraham, was communicating with Brandenburg the night he joined our little family. But I'll never know.

Since then, Ike has taken to barking. He's our first barking dog. But Ike is garrulous. He warns us against cats, songbirds, strangers and the approach of the supper hour.

Ike has two constants: He is always hungry and muddy. He is long-legged and ungainly, a puppy with big, floppy feet, and he can't bear the sight of a bucket brimming with water.

I fill the bucket each morning, Ike promptly knocks it over and spills the contents. Then he burrows into the mud. Every time I pass within range of Ike he greets me fondly and I require a change of slacks.

Nobody is more appreciative of Ike than our friendly local cleaning establishment.

We don't have to whistle for Ike, we just follow his footprints. I am considering installing a windshield wiper on the partly glassed door where he peers into the house and pleads for admission.

One day, no doubt, Ike is going to be a splendid retriever. Already he has displayed an aptitude for retrieving; he brings us old tomato cans, frayed slippers, cushions from the patio furniture, and bits and pieces of the garden hose.

He provides an element of suspense previously lacking. In times past my wife would greet me at the end of the working day with a smile and a hug and, sometimes, a glass of water flavored with scotch.

Now she usually remembers to smile before she asks, "Guess what YOUR dog did today?"

I know she doesn't mean Abe. And I can guess, without being told, that he's been poking in the trash barrels again. Once he swallowed a bird killed by Heathcliff, the mischievous black tomcat.

"Swallowed it with one gulp," my wife reported. I couldn't decide if she was distressed, or impressed.

Abe has become thinner, and that was part of the plan in adopting the puppy. But he's also less complacent. Ike is competition. When I seek to show affection to Abe, the puppy intrudes.

I stroke Abe's old gray head and Ike clamors for attention. He pushes against my legs, sits on my feet. If I persist in petting Abe, the puppy gently takes my wrist between his teeth and removes my arm.

Of course, Isaac is irresistible. In the evening I sit on the stoop to watch him eat, to make sure that he gets an equitable portion, and when he's finished he crawls into my arms and presses his nose against my neck while his tail waggles furiously.

I don't know if Ike is doing anything to postpone Abe's retirement, but he brightens my days.

Ike Loses His Innocence

I had sought to counsel Isaac, Son of Abraham, to beware of cats carrying mice. But Ike, being young and headstrong, was determined to make his own mistakes.

It was around three o'clock in the morning when Ike encountered a black and white kitten during his nocturnal meanderings.

They met under a shrub under our bedroom window. The cat reacted to Ike like Charlie Finley being introduced to Bowie Kuhn.

I'm sure we'll never have to fumigate our home for termites.

That skunk released enough gas to fly the Goodyear blimp to Pittsburgh. The atmosphere was suffocating. When I awakened, the odor had filled our bedroom, the entire house. My wife was sitting up in bed, holding a handkerchief to her face.

The place was under siege. It was nature's version of biological warfare, and we had lost.

Even now, several days later, the odor clings to the shrubbery — and to Ike.

Issac is a Labrador Retriever of seven months and a lovable little chap most of the time. He needs and demands affection, he is happiest when he can snuggle into your arms and fasten himself to your chest.

Right now he has to be content with a kind word. I know Ike feels rejected, but I'd rather hug a 500-pound gorilla than a pup who has been consorting with skunks.

We admit his sire, Abe of Spoon River, to the house while Ike regards us with a steady gaze. Abe chuckles in his gray beard. Long ago, he learned to avoid cats equipped with tear gas.

I imagine Ike had decided that when you've seen one cat, you've seen them all. He is accustomed to heckling our resident tom, Heathcliff. Heath will spit and scratch, but he doesn't brace his feet and lift his tail.

Actually, Heathcliff doesn't do much of anything since he became smitten with a ball of fluff down the street, a calico cat who goes about with bells on her collar and other fancy airs.

Heathcliff thinks she is beautiful. But, alas, his love is unrequited.

Heath has been losing weight alarmingly, and we feared he had contracted a dreadful disease. But our friendly animal doctor has concluded Heath suffers from an affliction of adolescence. He is love-sick.

The diagnosis came just in time to spare our dwindling supply of firewood.

Our resident house nurse has had a fire blazing on the hearth night and day since Heathcliff's health became a concern. Tenderly, she preheats a blanket and places it before the fireplace and there Heath resides, dreaming of the calico cat.

Until we learned the nature of Heath's problem, my wife had ministered to that lovesick cat with every thing from a croup kettle to chicken soup.

Indeed, he is a tragic figure. He is so skinny you can

feel his ribs when he crawls on your lap, whimpering softly. His coordination is awful. Any cat can land on his feet, but not Heathcliff. He fell off the washing machine and alighted on his head.

His morale is such he has even lost interest in boxing. Until love struck him, Heath's favorite recreation was sparring with the lady who prepares his chicken soup. She would slip on the heavy work gloves she wears while working in the garden, and the two would get down on the living room rug for a lively encounter.

But no more. Heath just drowses before the fire, his long black tail curled about his pointy black head. He pecks at his food and when he goes out he sits on the stoop and mopes.

The animal doctor assures us Heathcliff will recover, that lovesickness among tomcats is rarely fatal. We are hopeful and, meanwhile, we're becoming nervous about that calico cat, that fickle feline, who doesn't respond to the attentions of our handsome tom. Clearly, she is unworthy of such devotion.

I pray that problem will be speedily resolved. The firewood is going fast — and I'm getting awfully tired of warmed over chicken soup.

'I Wanted to Break His Neck'

When we entrusted Isaac, Son of Abraham, to the care of a professional dog trainer, one of the neighbors got the idea we had sent him to an obedience school.

"Let me know how it goes," he requested, "I may want to enroll a couple of kids."

Ike is a spirited Labrador Retriever of nine months who is a greater threat to the blooms of nature than fire. My wife, bleakly regarding her ravaged flower beds, termed him an ecological disaster.

Thus, Ike was introduced to Ramon Alvarado, tutor of hunting dogs. In time they would develop a splendid relationship, but Ramon was not so pleased with Ike in the beginning.

"Jack, to tell you the truth," he said, "I wanted to break his neck the first week."

Fortunately, he resisted this impulse. Ike wasn't incorrigible, he had been spoiled by a chickenhearted master. I had given him affection but not much discipline.

"This puppy is just a pet," groused Ramon, "all he wants to do is play."

But Ramon has motivated him. At last he is beginning to behave like a dog with a long history of field champions in his line. He may even become a worthy successor to his sire, Abe of Spoon River.

After six weeks, Ike's marks are much better. He is conscientious about obeying commands and he makes fine retrieves both on land and in water.

"Jack," says Ramon warmly, "Ike is one terrific dog. In the water he is amazing."

Yet Ike is seriously flawed. He is gun-shy. When Ramon fires a pistol, Ike cowers under a car. This is not the reaction one seeks from a gun dog. I have no skill with a bow and arrow.

"Jack, do not worry," counsels Ramon, "I will teach Ike not to fear guns. He will need time. You cannot hurry a puppy; we must be patient with Ike."

We are prepared to be patient. Especially my wife and Abe. I do not see Abe wearing a lachrymose expression since Ike went off to boarding school because, for one thing, his house privileges have been restored.

Abe had been excluded while Ike was in residence. You can't admit one dog and leave the other outside, his nose against the door. Thus, we had two Labs on the stoop and those dogs have such imploring eyes.

Now Abe is back in the bosom of the family, his companionship is welcome. When I am stuck for a thought and push back the chair to stare out the window, he seems to understand. He sits beside me and we wait together for inspiration. A man hitched to a typewriter deserves moral support, and Abe provides it.

When a thought comes along Abe goes back to sleep and I resume my three-finger typing.

There was a time when men assumed their sons would follow them as bankers, attorneys, chefs or violin makers, carrying on the family name, the family's business. I had disappointed my own father, who educated himself in law and then found excitement in Oklahoma searching for oil. It was his plan that I would become a petroleum engineer.

But I had no vocation for oil or anything involving mathematics. I was no more fitted for petroleum engineering than the role I mistakenly assigned to Isaac, Son of Abraham.

Just as I was sure my own son would crave knowledge and education, I never doubted that Ike would be a fine hunting dog. When I drifted into fantasy, I even visualized him as a field trail champion.

Ike, I must admit, is another example of my flawed handicapping.

I once picked the loser in a two-horse race. I was positive Jimmy Carter would vanish after the New Hampshire primary. I knew Muhammad Ali couldn't beat George Foreman in Zaire even if he had a witch doctor in his corner.

My latest miscalculation is Isaac. I chose him from a litter of eight pups, seven males and a female, sired by my distinguished Labrador Retriever, Abe of Spoon River. I picked a stiff.

As the owner of the sire, I had my choice of the litter.

Hindsight tells me I should have sought counsel from an expert. There are people who can look at a dog or a horse and divine the qualities of a champion. Jay Odell, who has bred Labradors for 50 years, has this skill. So does Bob Jordan, a game warden and naturalist whose knowledge of Labradors often dazzles me.

But I decided to trust my instincts. I looked over a mass of squirming black puppies and picked up a little fellow who caught my eye because he was so busy in the pen.

"I'll take this one," I told my daughter, "his name is Isaac, Son of Abraham. He will be a great dog because he is the issue of Abe."

I forgot that breeding doesn't guarantee quality. Rich men pay $300,000 to take their mares to Secretariat but it will be astonishing if the red horse repeats himself.

Some argue that Franklin and Eleanor Roosevelt formed the most illustrious union of the 20th Century America, but their progeny will have only a footnote in history. The five Roosevelt children have been party to 17 marriages, they have known scandal, controversy and unhappiness. FDR was the last statesman of his line.

Yet I innocently believed that any son of Abe's would be a retriever worthy of the sire. And worthy of — please excuse the expression — the bitch. Tara, Abe's mate, is a titled lady who comes from Odell's Consort Kennels in Illinois. She has splendid credentials.

In selecting Ike, I used the scientific method I practice when invited to serve as a judge at a beauty contest. He was the most handsome pup of the lot, I chose him unhesitatingly.

Ike has become part of my education. As a small boy, I learned that corn silk makes a rotten cigarette. As a young man, I discovered that if you mix beer and bourbon it makes a concoction known as a boilermaker and it gives you a headache. Now I find that there is an art to selecting a hunting dog.

The lesson left me lighter in the wallet. I entrusted Ike to the care of Ramon Alvarado, a kindly man, a trainer of excellent reputation. It is said of Ramon that he is especially gifted in working with young dogs because he has lived 80 years and most of that time he has devoted to schooling hunting dogs.

In the beginning, Ramon was optimistic about Ike. He encouraged me to observe while he instructed Ike in the basic business of retrieving. He taught him to find a training dummy in brush and to make long retrieves in a lake near his home.

The schooling continued for four months and, as time passed, Ramon became apprehensive. The first signal came when he politely suggested that my presence was distracting. Ike wanted to romp and play when I appeared; he ignored Ramon's commands. So it was agreed I would stay out of sight until Ike was more serious about his work.

Well, as we all know, college isn't for everybody. Ike no more wanted to become a hunting dog than I aspired to be a petroleum engineer. Ike is a dropout.

Or, more accurately, he was expelled when Ramon finally lost patience.

The phone rang at the office and I heard the rich Latin accent of Senor Alvarado.

"Jack," he said, "you must come and get Ike; I can't keep him no longer."

"Why, Ramon? What is the problem?"

"I will explain when you come for him. Goodbye, Jack."

I went for Ike later in the day. Ramon greeted me with a solemn expression.

"Jack," he said, "this dog is no good. He will not retrieve, he is gun-shy, he is wasting your money. Ike is only a pet. If you want my advice, get rid of him.''

This was difficult, we had become very fond of Ike. But we made arrangements to place him with a man who asks nothing of a dog but friendship. Ike became the companion and ward of a Catholic monk, Brother Andre, and they lived happily ever after.

That, at least, is what I want to believe. We learned that Brother Andre had been transferred to a monastery in the east and Ike had gone with him.

Naturally, Ike was wearing a Roman collar.

Chapter 6

WOMAN'S BEST FRIEND

Those who'll play with cats must expect to be scratched.

Miguel de Cervantes

It's not that I dislike cats, but I've always been partial to dogs. I tried to explain this to Heathcliff when he jumped into my lap and began purring loudly.

"Cat, why don't you get lost," I protested, "you're spilling my gin."

Heathcliff ignored my command. He climbed atop my chest, snuggled his head under my chin, and went to sleep.

I had a chance to get acquainted with Heathcliff while recuperating from a minor illness diagnosed by the neighborhood witchdoctor as the flu. The witchdoctor prescribed antibiotics and gin, and I predict he will go far in the medical profession. Of Heathcliff, I am less confident.

He is a small, lively black tomcat of undistinguished lineage who came to us as a gift from my daughter. He was named by my son, John Patrick, and his function, as

I understand it, is to provide atmosphere. My wife fancies the sight of a cat curled before the fireplace and through the years we have acquired dozens of the creatures for this purpose. Naturally, they were totally uncooperative.

Until Heathcliff. He's fascinated by the leaping flames and he finds it exciting to paw at the metal curtain which guards the fireplace. Eventually he tires of this game, curls up before the fire, and goes to sleep.

Then Patricia purrs. Patricia is my wife.

She is delighted with Heathcliff and we all find him very amusing, with the possible exception of Abe of Spoon River. Abe is a gentle Labrador Retriever, he has the disposition of a saint. In his secret heart, he regards the little tomcat as an interloper. But he is gracious, he conceals his resentment.

Abe could swallow Heathcliff with one bite, but he doesn't even growl when the cat playfully stands on his hind feet and caresses his face. That's when I fear for Heathcliff's safety. Wait until he tries that maneuver on the German shepherd up the street; he'll get zapped.

Still, the cat might be useful while he lasts. Abe has fetched me a lot of columns in recent years, not to mention quail, pheasant, chukkar and other delectables. I expect less from Heathcliff.

For one thing, he's addicted to television. I turn on the set to watch a football game and Abe takes a nap. But Heathcliff is a football nut.

I don't know what he thinks of the strategy, but he takes a keen interest in the game. He sits on my lap, ears pricked, watching intently. Then he sees something on the screen — a mouse trap play, perhaps — and he leaps to the sofa for a closer view. Occasionally he paws at the images on the TV screen.

No doubt this is a serious flaw in his character, but I don't propose to reform him. What was it that Eugene McCarthy said about politics and football? You have to be smart enough to play the game but dumb enough to think it's important.

My wife says I am wrong in dismissing Heathcliff as a TV degenerate. His interest in football disputes the research of authorities who contend that TV holds no attraction for animals. Heck, this little cat is interested in anything that moves.

When he saw his reflection in a mirror, he immediately began sparring with the enemy.

He may need that competitive spirit. There are a number of large, mature toms in the neighborhood and they've been prowling about the premises in a hostile mood. Fortunately, Heathcliff is quick. Blink an eye and you'll miss him as he shinnies up a pepper tree.

Sometimes I wonder if Heathcliff is using all nine lives at once. I see him on the balcony, the garage roof, in a tree, everywhere. In repose, he's apt to be sleeping at Abe's feet. At other times he amuses himself by climbing atop the sofa and chewing on my hair.

The cat fancies himself a hunter. This we learned when he killed a sparrow and deposited it on the sofa. I'll thank him to leave the retrieving to Abe.

I guess old Abe knows the cat doesn't represent real competition. Abe's place is secure. But the cat has some illusions. When Abe comes to my chair and leans against me and I softly stroke his beautiful head, the cat displays jealousy.

Suddenly Heathcliff appears, leaps on my lap and begins arching his back in a threatening manner. He is belligerent and possessive and he looks as though he is considering the idea of pouncing on Abe's back.

Fortunately, he restrains that impulse. Abe is the most lovable chap of my acquaintance but I wouldn't want him tested in this manner. As I keep reminding Heathcliff, I'm a dog man myself.

There is an art to loafing and I like to think I have mastered it. The idea is to be active without doing anything constructive, worrisome or worthwhile. By my wife's testimony, I am an accomplished loafer.

In all modesty I am prepared to claim my latest vacation was an unqualified success. Two weeks of rest and rehabilitation vanished as rapidly as a long weekend. Twelve of the 14 days were given over to hunting in the company of Abe of Spoon River and other congenial types. Most of the remaining time was devoted to gazing into a cheery fireplace and observing the peculiar behavior of Heathcliff, the clumsy cat.

Heathcliff is a black tom kitten who recently was assigned to our care and I have come to regard him with growing astonishment. All my life I have been conditioned to believe that cats are the most graceful of domestic animals. Feline grace, and that sort of thing.

Not Heathcliff. I'm prepared to submit that the phrase bull in a china shop is a misnomer. More accurately, it's cat in a china shop. Or Heathcliff among the crockery.

I suspect Heathcliff could get hurt stepping off a curb. I saw him topple from a fence. I watched him leap for a bee in a window, lose his balance on the window sill, and tumble to the floor. Twice he rolled over while sleeping on my lap and landed, crash landed, at my feet.

"I don't think he's really a cat," said my wife, "he doesn't act like a cat."

But he looks and sounds like a cat. He purrs. He bites, he scratches, he talks like a cat. He curls himself in a ball before the fireplace and, during his wakeful moments, he catches birds and climbs trees.

I wish he'd stay out of trees. To Heathcliff, trees are a one-way street. He goes up but he won't come down. Once aloft, he perches on a tree limb and cries piteously until a rescuer arrives. That's me.

I'm getting a bit long in the tooth to be shinnying up trees. It's not as easy as it used to be, and not as much fun. But Heathcliff never gets himself marooned in a tree if my agile, long-legged son is about the premises. I guess he likes excitement and suspense.

There's considerable drama when I climb atop a stepladder, reach for a low-hanging branch, and begin hoisting myself up a tree trunk. Meanwhile, my wife contemplates imminent widowhood.

"You'd better come down," she cautions, "before you break your fool neck."

But no, I'm determined. I remember the rallying cry of the late Vincent Lombardi: "The harder you work, the harder it is to surrender."

Ultimately, I descend with Heathcliff. And the trip down is the worst part. Regrettably, I have neglected to wear gloves. Heathcliff is alarmed and he expresses his concern by biting the nearest object. My right hand.

That's gratitude. "That," I tell my wife, "is why I am a dog man. Abe would never bite me if I rescued him from a tree. Come to think of it, I've never seen Abe climb a tree."

Yet I have to admit he had a certain glint in his eye when I left him over a weekend for some duck and pheasant hunting in northern California. We had been together day after day, in pursuit of a buckskin or a covey of quail, and now I was compelled to leave him behind.

That Labrador has the most accusing eyes, and I didn't know how to explain. It would be a commercial flight to Sacramento and then a charter to Venice Island in the Delta country near Stockton, and Abe wouldn't fit in my luggage. We arrived in the air taxi chartered by my adventurous friend, Bill Black.

We landed smoothly in the gathering darkness and we could just see the ground in the dim light. Joe, one of the club's employes, was impressed.

"Mr. Black," he said, "that's about the latest I've ever seen anybody land on this island."

Five minutes later the darkness was total. As total as our contentment. I always accept eagerly when Black invites me to rough it at Venice Island. The conditions are rather primitive — Gus, the chef from the San Francisco Hilton, served such plain fare as Dover sole, lamb chops, bouillabaisse and, incredibly, Long Island duck. At other times, we snacked on caviar, shrimp, frog legs and king crab.

Bill Black, as you can see, needs no lessons in the art of leisure. He also wooed the birds to the blind and shot most of them. Then he generously credited the marksmanship to others. Is there a better definition of class?

He Wears Abe's Perfume

My old dad used to say if you lie down with skunks, you'd better plan on changing clothes out in the garage. But I don't think he knew much about skunks.

Heathcliff, our clumsy cat, consorts with skunks. But he smells like a dog.

Heathcliff is a rumpled black tomcat who will never be domesticated in the strictest sense. He has the wisdom to prefer the company of animals to the society of people.

Occasionally we see him romping in the canyon below our hillside scatter with the resident skunks. Their relationship evidently is congenial because Heathcliff never returns with a skunky odor.

His favorite companion, however, is a black Labrador Retriever, Abe of Spoon River. To Heathcliff, Abe is absolutely irresistible. Wherever Abe goes about the premises, Heathcliff is never far behind. Sometimes Abe is so indulgent he allows the clumsy cat to sleep on his back. Abe snores, Heathcliff purrs.

At first, my wife thought this was terribly cute. Then she became aware of Heathcliff's new fragrance.

"You are a strange cat," she told Heathcliff, "you smell like a dog."

It is the custom of the cat to snuggle on my wife's shoulder as a declaration of love and devotion. Now she receives him with diminished enthusiasm.

"When a cat smells like a dog," she observes, "it certainly doesn't make him more attractive."

Being an experienced husband, thoroughly domesticated and housebroken, I resist an impulse to speak in Abe's defense. But, secretly, I am annoyed.

Maybe Abe smells like a dog but he is beautiful. And smart. And well-mannered.

The cat has never retrieved anything worthwhile, unless you count sparrows and Christmas tree ornaments. I don't know how many times I chased that fool cat out of the Christmas tree.

The cat comes running when he hears the sound of the electric can opener but he is undisciplined. He won't sit on command and politely await an invitation to enter the house. No. He dashes between your legs and he goes the most unlikely places.

Once he disappeared and I finally located him in the liquor cabinet. He doesn't even know he's a cat. He'll stand on his hind legs and spar playfully with Abe, apparently believing he is a Kodiak bear. At other times he thinks he is a bird. My wife found him sleeping in a thick growth of shrubs; he had made himself a nest and gone to roost.

Abe is neat and sleek and beautifully groomed. All his admirers say he is especially handsome when he wears his bright orange collar. Heathcliff is a hippie cat. He's always tousled and ill-kempt. He looks as though he had slept in his clothes.

Abe is gentle, sensitive, trustworthy and kind. He is what every Boy Scout aspires to become. Heathcliff is ornery, deceitful, lively and interesting. He has a mean face and a disposition to match. He is of uncertain parentage — I understand his father was a traveling salesman — and of doubtful character.

He knows I am a dog man but he doesn't deceive me by smelling like a dog. I know that if I presume to stroke his fur he probably will savage my hand. I know that if I open the door for him he'll just sit there like a balky mule. Nevertheless, he is welcome because he isn't always predictable.

He's the only cat I've ever seen who watches airplanes in flight. He also is attracted to football on television and, of all things, water. When my wife works in the yard, he plays in the garden sprinkler. When I get naked in the shower, he follows me into the tub. At such times, he probably believes he is a Labrador Retriever.

Labs love water but, oddly, they dislike rain. When I am bird hunting with Abe he will leap into cruelly cold water, sometimes breaking through a coating of ice. He splashes about in water that would discourage a trout, submerging to the level of his chin, and his expression suggests pure bliss.

Abe has two dimensions, a hunting personality and a domestic personality. At home, he is appalled by a gentle rain. A few drops of water splatter the patio and he urgently demands shelter. He scratches at the door, whines piteously, and shivers with cold. If that doesn't work, he coughs.

Nobody would be so heartless as to leave a fine dog out in the rain at the risk of catching pneumonia.

Besides, how can a cat properly snuggle against a wet dog. The only thing worse than a wet dog in the house, my wife tells me, is a cat who smells like a wet dog. That's Heathcliff.

Beware of the Cats

The two kittens are about the size of a man's fist. One, the male, is black and white and it has the face of a panda. The other, a liberated female, is pearl gray and feisty.

The function of the kittens, if I understand correctly, is to discourage rattlesnakes.

This theory is advanced by my wife, who somehow acquired the cats shortly after we moved into our new home in the country.

As it happened, my brother was visiting at the time said spouse arrived with the kitten who resembles a panda. The kitten's name is Clovis.

"He'll take care of that rattlesnake," explained my wife in an authoritative tone.

My brother examined the tiny ball of fluff, then regarded the lady with disbelief.

"Patricia, my love," he said, "you gotta be kidding."

My brother goes about with the New York Mets, speaking into a microphone when the Mets play baseball, and goes home to a town house in Connecticut. In this environment, he has not learned much about cats and rattlesnakes.

"Why don't you get a mongoose, instead?" he asked.

Patiently, my wife explained the two kittens, Clovis and Clotilde, will empty the premises of gophers. The rattlesnakes, deprived of gopher meat, then will go elsewhere.

"Oh," said my brother. But I could see he was unconvinced.

No wonder. The kittens have a lot of growing to do before they can win two of three falls from a gopher. If, alas, I meet a rattlesnake I'm not going to whistle for Clovis and Clotilde. Not with a cabinet loaded with shotguns.

We've been sans cat since Heathcliff, the clumsy tom, expired of consumption. At least, it was a fatal disease.

I offered to get a replacement immediately but my wife, who makes all the important decisions, decided it would be better to wait until we had moved to our new home in the country. Cats don't travel well, she explained. They become disoriented.

This could be one reason I am partial to dogs. Abe of Spoon River, my Labrador Retriever, has no hangups about our new address. He climbed into the rear of the Jeep Wagoneer and fell asleep. Upon arrival, he jumped out, explored the place for a while, found my desk, curled under it, and went back to sleep.

But he isn't charmed by the kittens. They spit at him. Especially Clotilde. She gets her back up and hisses when Abe aproaches within 10 feet. Abe regards the creature with disgust. He's been part of the family for nine years. What's spitting at him, anyway? A mouse?

The names, Clovis and Clotilde, come from my son. The young man reads a lot and I guess he knows about French royalty. Or, maybe, the names are his revenge. He sneezes in the company of cats.

Having a clever, original turn of mind, I wanted to call the male Charlie. He has a white face and a black nose and puts me in mind of Charlie Chaplin. So he's Clovis.

For a period of about six hours, I wondered if we should have named him Judge Crater. Clovis just vanished. We searched everywhere but to no avail. I speculated he had been eaten by a gopher. But my wife wasn't amused. Indeed, she was alarmed.

Toward dusk, she found a small opening in the baseboard beside the dishwasher. The kitten, she decided, had climbed through the hole and was hiding behind the dishwasher.

"We'll have to get him out of there," she reasoned, "or he'll burn up when I start the dishwasher."

But how? I don't even know how to fix a typewriter ribbon.

My wife got down on her knees with a hammer and screwdriver and tried to remove the baseboard. No chance. I considered calling the fire department, a plumber, a carpenter, a priest. Failing that, I called a neighbor, a nice man named Len.

He knows how houses are constructed. And he knows

about cats. He removed a piece of the dishwasher and beamed a flashlight into the innards of the kitchen cabinet. No Clovis. Thank God.

We talked it over. I offered Len a drink but he declined. I made one for myself and wondered if cats are really necessary to save us from rattlesnakes.

Suddenly Len noticed a movement in the hallway. "And what have we here?" he asked.

Clovis, of course. A very small, sleepy kitten, mewing and thinking about his stomach. He'd been asleep in one of the closets, probably tucked in a boot or shoe.

But we all sleep more soundly knowing that Clovis and Clotilde are on the night watch.

It had seemed a fine day. We had flushed a large covey of quail from a thicket of sage and returned with a fair number. Abe of Spoon River came home wearing a grin and a feather on his chin.

But Clovis, the tomcat with a panda's face, was pouting. Clovis is a cat who wants to be a dog.

My wife had observed his frustration. "He's been picketing the place," she reported. "All day he's been circling the house, yelling for Abe."

We are astounded both by Clovis' behavior and his voice. When he came to us as a kitten he made weak mewing sounds and we believed him timid. Now he bellows like a rock star.

Clovis has the company of a black female named Clotilde, but he chooses the society of Labrador Retrievers. Abe is tolerant of this aberration. He allows Clovis to rub against him, and he offers no complaint when the cat curls into a ball and sleeps at his feet.

Often they go walking together. Now that we live in the country and confinement is unnecessary, Abe has freedom to roam and he walks about his domain in the manner of a mountain lion. This appeals to Clovis.

The two of them go along, side by side. A large black Labrador and a small cat with white feet and a long black tail which stands like an antenna. Abe's pace is leisurely; there are many fascinating scents to investigate and often it is necessary to sit and scratch a spell. Clovis waits good-humoredly.

The only conflict occurs if the cat comes too close when Abe is busy with supper. Then Abe gives off with a roar which starts in his chest and commands respect. Wistfully, Clovis watches him from a safe distance.

The other cat, Clotilde, is even more discreet. While Abe sups, she observes him from a window in the laundry room. Clotilde is afraid of the dark so we leave a light burning during the night while she sleeps in a laundry basket.

We gather up the cats at nightfall and lock them in the garage because they would make a tasty meal for the neighboring coyotes. The coyotes are an unseen presence, and their numbers are unknown. 'Tis said a pair of coyotes can make more music than a dozen barbershop singers. We hear them yipping most nights and I think I hear enough voices for an opera. But they do not send shivers along my spine. I like the idea of sharing the place with wild creatures.

My wife is the one who shivers. She hears the cry of the coyote and becomes very protective about her cats. But she is comfortable in the country.

The sound of a great horned owl or the trill of a meadowlark fills her with delight. Lately she has been excited about the arrival of a pair of bluebirds, an event almost equal to her discovery of a golden eagle standing watch in a eucalyptus tree.

When the eagle soars overhead, his wings glinting in the sun, my wife snatches up binoculars and regards him with purest pleasure. He is much more beautiful, she has decided, than our other visitors, including the red-tailed hawk.

I find myself wondering if she would do harm to the female cat if it molested the bluebirds. Clotilde is a hunter. While Clovis goes walking with Abe, Clotilde stalks lizards or crouches in the tomato plants, hoping to pounce upon an unwary songbird.

Thus far, she has had little success. But the new bird-bath offers exciting possibilities.

The birdbath is my wife's welcome to the bluebirds. And the response has been cordial.

I was watching a football game on a TV screen when my wife burst into the study. Her face was alight with triumph.

"Who do you suppose were the first to use the birdbath?" she asked.

"The bluebirds?"

"Yes, yes, come and see."

I left the football game for a spell to watch the bluebirds at the baths. They seemed pleased with my wife's gesture of friendship. The male, with his rosy breast, struck me as a handsome sort. If Clotilde chases him, I'll be cross with the cat.

I don't believe Clotilde is much of a threat. She is clumsy and slow, and no wonder she is afraid of the dark. She falls off chairs and door screens and lands on her head. When she runs, she has a peculiar get-along. Her sides jiggle like saddle bags.

Clovis and Clotilde were acquired to save us from gophers and ground squirrels, and they must be doing something right. We had a bountiful harvest of zucchini, tomatoes, eggplant and pumpkins. Only the bell peppers were a failure.

My wife knows almost everything, but she can't explain about the bell peppers. She spoke to the plants in a tender voice and sang pretty tunes to make them happy. But they sulked like Clovis when Abe goes hunting.

I wonder if the bell peppers are tone deaf.

The Love Marks of Clotilde

Love is reading her horoscope first or speaking tenderly to a Labrador Retriever who awakens you by shaking his choke chain before the morning paper hits the driveway or the milkman begins his daily rounds.

Any man addicted to hunting knows only half the pleasure of this activity if he is without a good dog. Abe of Spoon River, my companion for 11 years, fits that description.

But he doesn't seem to know or care that I am a night person, a light sleeper and, hopefully, a late sleeper.

He welcomes dawn like a coyote. Eagerly and noisily. Given a choice, I'd rather be awakened by a clock radio or a meadowlark singing an aria.

Instead, my day begins with old Abe in a darkened room at my bedside, rattling his chain like a cowbell. His tail is swishing, his feet are dancing, his eyes gleam with mischief. I wonder how he can be so cheerful when I am groggy with sleep. I suspect his watch is set on eastern time.

Still, he's a grand old dog and I suffer his foolishness gladly. In most other ways, he is sensible, even considerate. Unlike our gelded tomcat, Clovis, he doesn't eat peanut butter and get his teeth stuck. I contend we made a bad choice in naming that cat Clovis.

I want to call him Luigi. His taste runs to Italian cuisine. His idea of a real delicacy is bread dipped in olive oil.

Yet I pefer Luigi to our other cat, a black female known as Clotilde. Clotilde is loving and all that, but she is afflicted with agoraphobia. She finds our red tile roof irresistible but there is nothing of Evel Knievel in her makeup. What goes up won't come down.

I don't really need the excitement of rescuing a cat from the roof at midnight. But this is often necessary because the cat is often on the roof. And danger lurks without. My wife worries when she hears the yipping of coyotes in a nearby pasture. Thus, nobody sleeps until Clotilde is safe in her bed in the garage.

Clotilde yearns to be rescued but displays her appreciation in a strange manner. She comes down scratching and clawing. My hands look as though I've been captured by a blackberry bush. I make frequent appointments for tetanus shots.

But we're learning to cope with Clotilde's fear of height. When I retrieve the neurotic cat I dress like a beekeeper — gloves, heavy jacket and a hat. My wife holds the stepladder and I grab the cat. Or vice versa.

Abe and the cats are the subject of this essay because I have had several inquiries lately about the health and well being of our pets. Especially Abe. There is an impression that Abe, who has been appearing in these pieces for more than a decade, is old, toothless and senile.

Not so. Abe is very senior for a hunting dog but he's a spry codger. He still goes hunting, he still does a fine job, and he can pass the fitness test. Most of the time he can leap on the tailgate of the Jeep in one bound, though occasionally I give him a boost. When he is weary after a long day in the field I gather him into my arms and lift him into the Jeep. He suffers this indignity without a whimper.

They say the legs go first on an old ballplayer, and that's equally true of a hunting dog. Abe has lost a few steps and he can't compete for a bird with Bob Jordan's dog, Jay.

If Jay were human, he'd be a ballplayer. He's young and eager and he can catch anything. On a recent day we went dove hunting and I was witness to Jay's remarkable agility; Bob shot a bird and Jay grabbed it before it hit the ground.

It figures. Jay has some human characteristics. For one thing, he sleeps with his head on a pillow.

And he knows more English than some college graduates. When it's time to retire for the evening, Bob's wife, Marian, addresses the dog as though he were a child: "Jay, are you ready to go nitey night?"

If the suggestion pleases Jay, he yawns.

If the idea is premature, he opens one eye, closes it quickly and pretends not to notice.

I am intrigued by the mannerisms of animals. Abe, for example, displays affection by sitting on my feet and leaning against me with one paw in the air. He likes to hold hands.

Jay is more rowdy. If he likes you, he shows it by rushing between your legs, usually from the rear. This can have interesting results when he gets sweet on a lady in a floor-length dress.

If Jay considers you a special friend, he grabs you by the wrist, not biting hard but sometimes hard enough to leave love marks. His boss, Bob Jordan, bleeds a lot.

Abe's manners are impeccable, if you discount the dirt he leaves on the hallway walls and the puffs of hair he sheds. He is so gentle I used to think he'd lick a burglar's hand but I've heard that deep growl in his throat. That's reassuring, and I'm glad to have his company.

A Mighty Hunter Is She

The resident horticulturist is consumed with outrage because small, unloved creatures come uninvited to her winter garden, order the Bill Walton Vegetarian Special, and leave without paying the check.

The peas are under seige, the lettuce is in tatters, and the abused gardener complains we have the best fed gophers and rabbits for miles around.

I don't know why this should be because we have sworn and deputized two lowborn cats, Clovis and Clotilde, to defend milady's pea patch.

At least, that was the theory. Our Secretary of Agriculture often says she is pragmatic about domestic animals. She is not a cat lover; only cats love other cats. Cats are useful; they are loyal, brave and true — and hungry. Only the most reckless or desperate rodent or rabbit would dare trespass with Clovis and Clotilde walking their beats.

But we are disillusioned by Clovis. He wouldn't fight a field mouse. Once he miscalculated and caught a gopher and the little beast bit him on the nose. Clovis dropped the gopher, uttered the feline version of profanity, and sought shelter in the nearest tree.

It is the gardener's theory that only a thin line separates domesticated cats from wild creatures, and I would not dispute such wisdom. Rather, it is more prudent to say that Clovis is the exception who proves the rule.

His notion of adventure is to lounge on my lap while the afternoon sun streams through the sliding glass doors and clack his teeth at passing songbirds.

Clovis is the Walter Mitty of gelded cats. He doesn't harm any living creature but his heart is full of malice. When the bluebirds sip at their drinking fountain, Clovis wiggles his little pointy ears, switches his tail, and grinds his teeth.

What he really wants is curb service. He'd be delighted if the lady who feeds him would catch a bird and bring it to him on a tray.

We don't have to be reminded that females are the hunters of the cat family. Clotilde is a cat who looks as though she bought her wardrobe at a rummage sale, then dressed in the dark. But she is industrious, and ferocious.

Clotilde would be even money against a leopard.

She kills something — a rabbit, a gopher, a bird —

almost every day. We are indebted to Clotilde for what remains of the winter garden.

If it weren't for Clotilde our carrots would be salad for gophers and we'd have rabbits the size of coyotes.

Clotilde dresses in black and, when hunting, has a disposition to match. I once saw her carry a full-grown rabbit into the yard, and the captive seemed larger than the hunter. Somehow Clotilde scaled a six-foot redwood fence and deposited the rabbit in the garage where she prefers to dine.

This kind of thing can result in a quarrel between Clotilde and the boss. When Clotilde tucks a napkin under her chin and prepares to eat a gopher on the door mat, she is admonished to mind her manners.

"Clotilde, you can't eat there," commands a stern voice.

The cat recognizes authority. Clotilde picked up the gopher, trotted across the garage, leaped to a table and placed her trophy in a plastic dish.

Being a gopher is a risky profession when Clotilde is around, but I am very much on the side of the cat. The gophers have killed four of our avocado trees, and I am convinced their only purpose is to feed cats, coyotes, weasels and gopher snakes.

We had a gopher snake for a while, and we were delighted to share his company.

Then a weasel arrived and we greeted him with glad cries. God put weasels on earth to destroy gophers, one of His better ideas.

The weasel was our most welcome guest since the peregrine falcons paused for a while, and then vanished into a trackless sky. The weasel was discovered by Clovis, and that was Clovis' bad luck.

Clovis is a trusting sort — actually, he's not very well informed — and he mistook the weasel for another cat of amiable temperament. The weasel was intent on murder.

Homicide was barely averted. The chief gardener beseeched, implored and yelled at Clovis to get the hell away from the weasel. But he insisted on a romp with the nice kitty.

Clovis owes his life to a garden hose. The lady grabbed the hose, turned the faucet on full bore, and squirted Clovis in the whiskers. Clovis scrammed.

Regrettably, the weasel vanished after two or three days. Maybe he was just a drifter passing through the neighborhood, a hobo in search of a handout.

This is what passes for adventure when one lives far enough from the city to be awakened by a chorus of meadowlarks as the sun warms the land and to hear the yipping of coyotes in the dark of night. The cats are locked in the garage and I'll wager that Clovis, secure in his bed, shivers when the coyotes wail. No doubt Clotilde answers with a growl.

The hand-lettered homily on the wall of Fern Heather's cheerful kitchen at Little Walker Lake in the serene High Sierra fitted my sentiments exactly: "Lord, Grant Me Patience — and I Want it Right Now."

Nearly two months had been consumed in mending from an inner ear infection, and even my doctor regarded me as an embarrassment.

The managing editor had ordered the daily publication of a small notice which explained that my absence was due to illness and, moreover, that my column would resume when I had healed.

But the ear specialist was becoming almost as uncomfortable as his patient.

"My other patients are asking why you are so slow in

recovering," he explained. "Couldn't the notice be changed to say that you are recuperating?"

This was quickly accomplished. The doctor is a decent sort, competent, good-humored and compassionate, and I felt guilt over such a protracted convalescence. The doctor deserved a more cooperative patient.

It was during this period I had been reading Fawn M. Brodie's superb biography of Thomas Jefferson, who confessed, "I am always mortified when anything is expected from me which I cannot fulfill."

Yet, this is a sword which cuts two ways. Though I was loath to embarrass my physician, it was pleasing to disappoint those who became persuaded I was rowing against the current on the river Styx.

The gossip reached me at June Lake, where we had gone in pursuit of trout and solitude, when an acquaintance phoned to ask about my well being. He had learned, he said, that I was in the last stages of a terminal illness.

His logic fascinated me. "I read that you were ill," he said, "Then I saw that you were on vacation. I assumed the rumor must be true."

Actually, I was in better shape than our neurotic tomcat, Clovis, who had lost a portion of his long curly tail to a coyote. Poor Clovis. He had carried his tail so proudly, twitching the white tip as a sign of affection. Clovis didn't walk, he strutted. He reminded me of the athlete who carries the flag in the Olympic ceremonial march. Now he's as bob-tailed as a Manx.

Yet, in our view he still makes a fine appearance. He is handsome and sleek and I take strong exception to the comments of a friend who complains that Clovis lacks style because he wears four white stockings. One is obliged to consider the source of such snobbery.

Clovis' critic is an occasional house guest who is variously known as The Torch and Smokey the Bear. He has a habit of drifting off to sleep with a lighted cigarette in his fingers. Which explains the asbestos blankets in our guest room.

I feel closer to Clovis than in times past because we are equally flawed by indolence. My typewriter has been stilled through much of the summer and thus, like Clovis, I have been much underfoot for that indomitable and cheerful woman, my wife, who keeps order in our home.

As the wife of the late George Weiss once observed, she took her spouse for better or worse — but not for lunch. It is worse than a curse to have a man about the house for days beyond count and I am prepared to offer testimony that togetherness is more overrated than certain baseball teams in the springtime.

Especially if the male is afflicted by a viral infection in the inner ear. This not only robs him of his strength and his sense of humor, but makes him sensitive about loud noise. He can't abide the clamor of a vacuum cleaner, a dishwasher or a power mower. He is of no demonstrated worth. Friends mow his lawn, his spouse struggles against sprouting weeds.

It is discomforting to participate in a discussion in which a wife evaluates the relative merits of a shiftless husband and a lazy Labrador Retriever. On reflection, I believe Abe of Spoon River got a little the worst of it.

He sheds his black hair on the floor in the kitchen, I leave mine in the shower. He rubs his oily black coat on the walls in the long hallway. I leave dirty towels. But Abe isn't much on conversation.

A husband can entertain by quoting from Oliver Wendell Holmes. Such as this splendid philosophy on bird shooting: "If you want to hit a bird on the wing, you must not be thinking about yourself and, equally, you must not be thinking about your neighbor; you must be living with your eye on that bird."

If this were an ordinary summer, I would quote the golfer-naturalist Billy Casper: "Every day a man goes fishing he adds a day to his life." But the summer was squandered on healing. Now I dream of autumn and times of renewed robust health when the geese and ducks will come down from the north along with other Canadian tourists and quail will fill Abe's moist nose with their scent.

Then I shall heed the counsel of Justice Holmes. Now, on the orders of my physician, I am obliged to sit and watch the weeds grow. It's the first time I've ever had a license to loaf.

The house wrens have been robbing the string mop to insulate their nests, the roses are blooming, the sycamores and the liquid amber trees are leafy in their green dress, and we are very much taken with the texture of spring.

The meadowlark on the neighbor's farm knows only one tune, but it pleases him greatly. He sings it from the first light of day until the last.

Red-tailed hawks wheel in the sky, then stoop suddenly on blackbirds who shriek with alarm. A valley quail, unaware of the danger, perches on a rock and calls loudly to his playmates. My wife admires the topknot of the rooster quail and Clotilde, the Ma Barker of domestic cats, scratches at the sliding glass door in her eagerness to stop the music.

Clotilde's fierceness charms us because this is proof a crisis has passed. She has survived the feline flu. Her health is restored, the best of gifts on Mother's Day.

Clotilde is a female cat of no special distinction. She is as common as mud, her dress is dowdy, her manners are slovenly. She is an affectionate cat who doesn't know how to sheath her claws. When Clotilde loves you, you feel it. She only hurts the ones she loves. Or eats.

But she has endeared herself to the lady who feeds her. When Clotilde developed the sniffles a certain tension possessed the house. We haven't had such trauma since a coyote tried to eat Clovis, our gelded male cat, and succeeded in bobbing his tail.

The sniffles were followed by a cough, though you have to know cats to recognize a cat cough. I thought she was sneezing. The cough was followed by many anxious phone conversations between Clotilde's keeper and the vet.

The vet, a kindly man named Frank Goldsmith, is accustomed to ministering to worried ladies who come to him with sickly cats. He examined Clotilde, determined she had a temperature of 103.5, stuck her with a needle, prescribed medication, and reassured her mistress.

Which is to say she went from panic to concern. The vet recognized the symptoms. In the event of an emergency, he would stand by for a summons. Even during the attitude adjustment hour. Even when the sun was below the yardarm. He promised.

Fortunately, the cat healed. But she took her sweet time, and no wonder. During the day she was comforted by a heating pad. At night she curled around a hot water bottle.

The cat had everything but a buzzer to summon the nurse. Clotilde isn't the brightest of animals but she enjoyed being pampered. Appendicitis victims make speedier recoveries.

There was talk of heating up the croup kettle but Clotilde evidently isn't enamored of steam. It was about that time she hopped off the heating pad, took a playful swipe at Clovis, clambered to a windowsill and displayed a fresh interest in the house wrens.

This was closely followed by a release of tension. The lady who had lovingly prepared a hot water bottle for her cat now regarded the beast less indulgently.

"I hate animals," she was heard to say, "I really despise all animals."

This exclamation came after Clotilde had resumed hunting and carried a rabbit into the garage. Clotilde will eat anything that doesn't eat her first. But she is messy. She leaves the head and other parts on a shag rug which covers the door stoop.

I wonder why this cat doesn't weigh 150 pounds. She feasts on rabbits, squirrels, gophers, birds and then comes to the door begging for supper. Yet she is mostly black hair and bones.

Clovis is an ornament; he is handsome and useless. But he is clever. He curls up beside his boss and presses his nose against her. Some find this irresistible.

Clovis is a bully with charm. He uses Clotilde as a punching bag and rousts her from her bed in the garage. But Clotilde thinks he's fascinating.

When Clovis climbs in with her — actually, he uses her for bedding in a small plastic basin — she responds by grooming his fur. Clovis never troubles to groom himself. Why bother? He just gets more handsome every day.

Clotilde would be more popular if she were less fastidious. She devotes more time to primping than a debutante. Clotilde is the sort who would leave a ring around the bathtub. She grooms herself by tearing great chunks of hair from her hide. I wonder if that hurts. I know it's not very neat. She leaves a trail of hair wherever she goes.

I am partial to Clotilde because she is feral and, therefore, she is interesting. She tolerates people, especially when they bring food and hot water bottles. But she doesn't need us, she accepts us.

That's a good relationship.

The wild animal who best accommodates himself to land developers and urban sprawl is the coyote who, strangely, fits comfortably into the society of man. Thus, we have the problem of coyote coping.

The coyote's idea of a gourmet meal is a domestic cat. Rare is the day when somebody doesn't ring the Department of Fish and Game or the Department of Animal Control, a county agency, to complain of cats being murdered by coyotes.

There is no statute which forbids the eating of cats by coyotes. The game wardens don't respond because protecting cats is not among their duties. The animal control people are philosophical about the peril of cats who, unable to find refuge in a tree, vanish suddenly without explanation.

I came across an item in a Fallbrook newspaper on coyote coping which put the matter in perspective. Somebody had interviewed Dr. Dean Thackrey, chief of San Diego County's health division in the Department of Animal Control.

"Nature is our principal means of coyote control," explained Dr. Thackrey, "they can multiply only as fast as their supply."

I suspect this is bureaucratic terminology for please don't feed the coyotes.

Dr. Thackrey notes that coyotes are attracted to any source of food and water. Especially cats. If you enjoy the company of small pets, especially cats, lock them in the house or garage when darkness approaches.

I am ambivalent about coyotes. I find pleasure in their nightly chorales, and I like to watch them run and play. Always there are coyotes about when one goes hunting. Sometimes we stare at each other with mutual interest, then we go our separate ways.

Lately, though, the coyotes have been making me nervous. They are becoming bolder, moving about in the daylight, sauntering ever closer to our home. This gives me concern about the safety of Clotilde, the black female cat who is very sporty in her new winter coat, and Clovis, the black and white tomcat.

Clovis already is living the second of his nine lives. A coyote got part of his black tail which featured a white tip. Clovis carried it with great dignity. Now he had only a stub. One of the neighborhood children found the missing part, put it in an envelope, and brought it to my wife. Children are sentimental, you know.

"Nature is full of predators and each one plays a part," reminds Dr. Thackrey.

So true. When we aren't worrying if the coyotes will feast on our cats, my wife frets about whether Clovis will eat her favorite rabbit.

The rabbit's name is Peter, which is not unusual, and he lives beneath a Rosemary bush. My wife and the rabbit have become quite chummy.

There are many rabbits about but this one is special because he has a red spot on his neck and he is company for my wife. They have long chats in the evening when the rabbit hops close, displaying no fear or concern. Indeed, he is so relaxed he stretches in the manner of a domesticated pet.

The rabbit also has no fear of Abe of Spoon River, a gentlemanly black Labrador. Abe ignores the rabbit because he had a proper upbringing. As a young hunting dog he was taught that chasing rabbits is unseemly behavior. Which is to say he tried it a few times and caught hell.

But Clovis has a keen interest in the rabbit. Most of the time this gelded tom with the abbreviated tail is just an ornament waiting to jump on somebody's lap. But the rabbit brings out the predator in Clovis.

He lies atop the back rest on the long couch in the living room and maintains a vigil. From the couch he has a fine view of the Rosemary bush, and he lies there, clacking his teeth and switching his tail.

Actually, he doesn't represent much of a threat. Clovis is just window shopping. It's my theory that if the rabbit jumped at Clovis he would flee and climb a tree. Clovis wouldn't go hunting without a knife or gun.

Nevertheless, my wife is anxious about the rabbit. When he comes out of the Rosemary bush at the cocktail hour, she gathers up Clovis and puts him under house arrest.

Then she fraternizes with the rabbit while Clovis, resentful and noisy, peers through the picture window.

Actually, the rabbit is lucky his presence hasn't been discovered by Clotilde. She hunts away from the house in nearby fields and meadows and she comes in just before dark, just ahead of the coyotes, with a full stomach. Clotilde can't eat all the rabbits but she's got 'em working nights.

Such is the balance of nature. One feral cat, one window shopping cat. And a hunting dog of impeccable manners.

Maybe you won't believe it when I say that Abe drinks in dainty fashion from a stone crock, then wipes his chin on a Juniper bush. Either he's awfully neat or he's fond of martinis.

Chapter 7

THE SPECIAL DAYS

If you pick up a starving dog and make him prosperous, he will not bite you. That is the principal difference between a dog and a man.

Mark Twain

There had been rain during the night and, in the mountains, the rain became snow. We had planned to cut a Christmas tree and the snow was a source of concern; I suspect the roads would be impassable.

I phoned my friend Bill, who lives near the mountain, seeking reassurance.

"Will the snow prevent us from cutting a tree?"

His tone was impatient. "I'll worry about that," he said. "Why don't you just think about something pleasant?"

I went back to my favorite chair and watched the oak logs blazing in the fireplace and visualized how the tree would look in the corner of the living room. The tree would displace the book table and surely it would be a grand sight.

One year I cut a tree and it was so dowdy my wife wouldn't let me bring it into the house. It seemed a splendid tree when we brought it off the mountain, but our vision was somewhat impaired by a scotch mist, and I had to agree it wasn't the best possible choice.

"It's the worst looking tree I've ever seen," said my wife, who has no reputation for understatement.

This time I was determined to be more discriminating. When we gathered at the foot of the mountain the following morning I explained to Bill the importance of locating a comely tree.

"Have no fear," said Bill, "I cut trees to match the personality of the owner. Your wife will be thrilled."

Still, I decided it would be prudent to take my coffee plain. The morning air was brisk and our breath made white vapors. A dollop of brandy would have been bracing, but I wanted to be sure.

We worked our way up the mountain with difficulty. A snowplow had been over the road but there was ice in the shady places and the pickup truck skidded and labored while Bill spun the wheel with studied non-chalance. There were four of us in the cabin of the truck and a black dog named Abe of Spoon River lay at our feet. Only Abe and Bill were breathing normally.

"First of all," said Bill, "you have to understand you are in the care of one of the world's greatest drivers."

He's pretty good, all right. We climbed the mountain without chains and without incident. Later the men with the snowplow came along and one of them called a greeting to Bill.

"I see you waited for a perfect day to cut a tree. Why would anybody want to come up here when it's nice and dry?"

Bill seemed not to notice. He was watching Abe chase madly about in the snow. Everybody feels younger in the presence of a new snow, and this storm had arrived during the night. Abe wasn't six years old any more, he was a puppy again. He dashed about in the snow, breathing the pure mountain air, and once he came running toward me pell mell and slithered between my legs.

The snow and Abe's black coat offered a vivid contrast I thought of Abe as the shadow of a Labrador Retriever who somehow had managed to become upright. But this shadow had been rolling on the ground for the sheer pleasure of it, and there were flecks of snow in his eyes and ears.

I saw the tree right away. It was beautifully formed and its branches were heavy with snow. A lovely tree; I wanted it very much.

"No," said Bill, "wait a while. I want to be sure."

I was sure. I waited beside the tree while Bill and the others searched the forest. It was a glorious morning on the mountain, and the cold and the snow and the hush among the trees made me think of Maria and Robert Jordan of "For Whom the Bell Tolls." I could smell the smoke of the campfire in the cave and taste the wine.

Here, in the stillness I heard only the voice of a bluejay and saw the track of a coyote and a rabbit. To the coyote, no doubt, the rabbit was a partridge in a pear tree. Then, among the trees, I caught the movement of deer, five of them, all fat, sleek and graceful. They made a fine sight against the snow but they bounded away in long strides when Bill and the others returned.

"You can have this one," said Bill of my tree, "it's a good choice. I'm sure your wife will let it in the house."

We took the tree and placed it carefully in the bed of the pickup truck, shaking some of the snow from the branches. Then we cut three other trees, all really good trees, and took them down the mountain with a sense of elation and accomplishment. The cutting of a Christmas tree is lovely tradition and I was thinking of a time when we decorated the tree with strings of popcorn and skated on the ponds until darkness forced us into the house, our cheeks tingling with cold.

The tree was a great success. My wife was so pleased with the tree I thought she was going to hug it, maybe pick it up and waltz it about the house. But she had a better idea. She hugged me, instead.

That Bill, he sure knows how to pick a tree that complements a woman's personality. And, in a way, he was saying a very nice thing about my wife. It is a beautiful tree.

The tree tilted a bit, and it wasn't very steady. But, for that matter, neither was Santa.

The lights glowed softly in the dusk and the ornaments reflected the blaze from a pair of Yule logs. We were very pleased with ourselves because the Christmas tree seemed especially beautiful this year.

"What would you say if I brought a tree of that size into the house in August?" I asked the co-owner of this community property.

She had been regarding the tree with a rapt expression. Now she regarded me strangely.

"I would say you are crazy," came the affectionate response.

The heir, a tall young man of 17, considered the idea only mildly impractical.

"I would say you are early," he suggested.

Ours is a very traditional family. We always have a tree and we need a big one because we have been acquiring ornaments for more than 20 years. My wife brought Christmas decorations as part of her dowry. There's a beautiful wreath on the door and a kissing ring in the entrance hallway.

I answer the doorbell ring and there stands the man from the cleaners, eyes closed, lips puckered.

"Cut it out," I warn him, "or I'll hit you with my purse."

Anyway, the tree is a triumph. It is tall and shapely with long, modest skirts down near the ankle and we steady it with a rope tied about the waist. The tree comes from a stand of virgin fir in the mountains, cut and delivered to our door by a friend. He also brings mistletoe for kissing rings, and such.

"It's the most beautiful tree we've ever had," says my wife, "and don't tell me I say that every year. We should celebrate — you can take me out to dinner."

Well, trimming the tree is one reason for eating out. Shopping is another. I think we had our last home-cooked meal on Thanksgiving Day. At my daughter's house.

Ah, well, 'tis the season to be merry and we bundle against the cold and go merrily into the night, guided by the bright light of the planet Jupiter, to our favorite bistro. There we find a merry old gentleman with flowing white chin whiskers, sipping VO and water through a straw and gently rubbing his corns.

"Ho, ho, ho," says the bearded old chap as my wife sits on his knee, "and what would you like for Christmas, little girl?"

She gets a whiff of the VO on his breath. "Santa," she asks, "why is it your perfume smells just like my husband's?"

This is the first Sicilian Santa we have encountered during the holidays. His true identity is John Pernicano and he comes from a place north of San Diego, La Jolla, to be exact.

Each year he puts on a red costume, straps on his chin whiskers, cushions his stomach with a pillow, and travels about the community in a Hertz rent-a-sleigh. He is a lovable old fellow and the children adore him. Most of them, that is.

One delightful little moppet tried to steal his boots

right off his feet. Another snapped his chin whiskers.

Now the hour is late, and Santa is happy but weary.

"First drink of the day," he says, eyeing the VO with appreciation, "you've got to play it straight with the kiddies. This Santa business is a gas."

Come to think of it, Santa is a privileged character. He has a license to flirt with pretty girls and even his wife can't object. If he were anybody else, the gendarmes would book him for prowling. Or nail him for double parking. Or impound his reindeer in the zoo.

And Santa is very influential. Most children are obedient and respectful in his presence. Santa tells then to clean their plates and drink all their milk, and they co-operate like little angels. Indeed, some are too co-operative.

One child holds her mother at the dinner table an extra hour because she is determined to drink all her 7-Up and please Santa.

"Santa, baby," pleads the mother, "tell the kid it's all right to leave or we may not get home for Christmas."

Santa enjoys his work. The little ones trust him and their eyes shine as they whisper their secrets in his ear. But sometimes they tug at his heart.

One little blonde with long curls and big eyes puts more faith in Santa than he'd like.

"I want my daddy home for Christmas," she says.

And where is daddy?

"He's a prisoner of the Viet Cong," says the child.

Santa is fighting back tears as he opens his big bag and invites the little girl to help herself to a doll and all the candy she can carry.

And in the evening, sipping his VO through a straw, he still thinks of the child. He needs that drink.

He Brings Home the Biscuits

The best part of the day was waiting for the hot rolls to come from the oven in the bakery at Tecate. The rolls are very tasty and a crowd gathers in the bakery at four o'clock each afternoon. The mood is something like that of a post-Christmas white sale. The aficionados of hard Mexican rolls are fiercely competitive.

We try to time our quail hunting in Baja California with the baker's schedule because the rolls disappear very rapidly. Going home without the fresh Mexican bread is regarded as a betrayal.

"How was the hunting?" asks the heir, politely.

"Just fair. We worked very hard, but the birds were scarce."

"Too bad," says the boy, "but did you bring the bolillos?"

The bolillos are the hard rolls from the Tecate bakery. The boy loves them. At 19, he is slender and hard-muscled and he can eat a dozen bolillos during an afternoon and he still looks fine. He is very enthusiastic about the rolls.

"Yes, I bagged five dozen bolillos, I think that is the limit during this season."

The boy was very pleased. He rewarded me with a pat on the shoulder.

"You are truly a great hunter," he said, "I'll bet you have no equal when it comes to bolillos."

This kind of thing passes for humor at our house. But there is a certain risk in competing for bolillos. When the pan comes from the oven piping hot at the Tecate bakery at four in the afternoon the customers are very aggressive. For quite a while, the demand exceeds the supply.

The bolillos are delicious and the price is right. Two cents apiece. Two cents plain.

Perhaps 20 people are clustered in the small bakery when the artist of the oven decides his creation is ready for purchase. The girl who works behind the counter peers into the kitchen, alert for a signal. The crowd is expectant and tense. There is a sensation of waiting for a glimpse of Liz Taylor's diamond.

The girl clerk is dressed in white, indicating the purity of the bread. Finally, the signal comes. She hurries into the kitchen and soon returns with a cardboard box. In the box are the precious bolillos.

The customers press forward eagerly. Some have trays and tongs provided by the bakery. Others hold brown bags and they snatch the bolillos from the box with their hands. Here is the element of risk. Put the hand in the wrong location and you get stabbed with a tong.

It takes fast hands to play this game. I managed to acquire 18 of the rolls from the first serving. Not bad, but it doesn't approach the Tecate record for free style bolillo catching. An old lady in a black shawl heaped her tray with at least three dozen of the rolls and I noted that she regarded me with pity.

Still, I did pretty well. I protected my tray when a young man tried to snatch it from me in an unguarded moment. When I glared at him, he smiled and shrugged. It's part of the game, senor.

After two servings, I had 36 of the rolls on two trays and I decided it would be unseemly to continue. I didn't want to be greedy. With my friend, Bob, I walked to the curb where the station wagon was parked and we opened a thermos of coffee and went after the bolillos while they were still fresh and hot.

It was a tasty combination and the aroma of the bread filled the station wagon. The two Labrador Retrievers in the rear of the vehicle were noisy and restive. I ate a bolillo and drank the coffee, and watched people coming out of the bakery. All of them carried brown bags and wore a triumphant expression.

"I think the crowd has thinned out now," I told Bob, "do you think it would be all right if I went back for more rolls?"

I had the uneasy feeling I might deprive a Tecate family of its evening meal.

"Go ahead," Bob encouraged me, "you don't have to feel guilty."

I returned to the bakery and the atmosphere was much more congenial. Only two customers, an old woman and a child, were waiting when the girl in the white smock came out of the kitchen with another batch of rolls. Deftly, I speared two dozen, and departed. It was like shooting fish in a rain barrel. Only better.

This was the only success of the day. We had exercised strenuously in pursuit of quail but we went to the wrong places. The dogs, Abe and Rip, flushed a few scattered birds but seldom more than four at a time. We couldn't find the coveys. Four men and four dogs hunted throughout the day and we shot only 10 birds.

We cleaned the quail and put them in a plastic bag, and left them in the wagon with two Labradors, a German shorthair and a Brittany spaniel while we went into a roadside bistro for a beer. The bartender lighted two Coleman lanterns and served the beer. We drank it with much pleasure.

Then we returned to the car and I reached under the seat to retrieve the birds. All that remained was a wisp of plastic. The spaniel had eaten the quail.

"You should have seen your face when you came up with that piece of plastic," said Bob, laughing, "it was beautiful."

At the border, the customs agent asked if we had anything to declare. He could see the guns and the dogs.

"Five dozen bolillos," I replied proudly.

Who says customs agents never smile?

Wildlife in the City

On this Easter morning the bird of peace sits on the nest high in the boughs of a eucalyptus tree. Meanwhile, the head of the family is much too nervous to read a magazine or watch the daytime TV programs.

He hops about from limb to limb, zealously guarding his mate. But she is cranky and demanding, and feels sorry for herself during confinements. Her hunger is constant. Every time he kicks off his shoes and begins to relax, she sends him to the corner delicatessen.

No doubt she is asking for something exotic. Limestone lettuce, perhaps. Truffles. Caviar. Papaya. But the papa dove is burdened with responsibility. He disappears briefly, and returns with an offering of love: a worm.

Watching this little domestic scene from our living room window, I am intrigued as always by the parallel struggles of man and nature. Here at Easter, a joyous time, the bird of peace is beset with problems.

For one thing, the neighbor's Siamese cat is crouched beneath the bird bath. That cat is no respecter of hunting seasons or city ordinances. If the dove alights for a drink or a bath, the Siamese will have squab for Easter dinner.

The cat has the patience and resolution of a horse-player. He crouches in the grass hour after hour, waiting for the dove to make a miscalculation. He reminds me of a smart hitter waiting for his pitch.

The cat knows that sooner or later the bird will become careless. And, now, he's especially vulnerable. He's been up late several nights in succession, struggling with income tax forms and the budget.

Once, searching for canceled checks, he almost tore the nest apart. No wonder they call them mourning doves.

Still, they seem a compatible couple. They fight infrequently and often they seem as happy as young lovers. Sometimes the old girl gets off the nest and the two of them take the sun on one of the tree branches.

This worries my missus. "Won't the eggs get cold?" she asked. "Isn't that mother bird shirking her duty?"

As one who eats a great deal in restaurants around the country, I am an authority on cold eggs. But I don't worry about them.

I tell the missus maybe the bird of peace has married a fry cook. I bet her pancakes are lousy, too. This does not bring what you would call a big laugh.

The papa dove is inscrutable. He reminds me of Bud

Grant, the unflappable Minnesota football coach. This bird does not take his responsibilities lightly.

Much of the charm of our little home in the west is the wildlife in the city. We share the grounds with foxes, skunks, gophers and a melange of birds that includes owls, red-tailed hawks, hummingbirds, stellars jays, finches, and a robin.

The owl used to sit in the tree where the doves now reside and make owl noises. Then he fell silent.

"I guess he just doesn't give a hoot," suggested the teen-aged bird watcher who answers, sometimes to the name of John Patrick.

The foxes and skunks have established quarters in a canyon at the foot of our backyard, and sometimes they go visiting. We recently observed one of the foxes hunkered in the street with two of the neighborhood dogs, and they seemed perfectly congenial.

The fox fled at the approach of our car, but the dogs merely regarded us with annoyance. They reminded me of old men who sit and gossip on the courthouse steps of small towns. I supposed they discussed the crops and the weather and the housewife who ran off with the traveling salesman.

We have established an uneasy truce with the skunks, a truce based upon mutual respect. Or fear. To paraphrase the late Will Rogers, I never met a skunk I didn't dislike. But we share the grounds in about the same manner Berlin is divided between east and west.

At first the creatures tormented my noble Labrador, Abe of Spoon River, by squirting him with tear gas. But Abe is much too mannerly to seek the company of such low types. Now he passes them without as much as a nod of acknowledgement.

Abe is a pacifist. A fat pacifist. This being between hunting seasons, a barren period, Abe hasn't been getting proper exercise and his profile suggests an absence of fasting during Lent.

Oh, well. If Easter is here, can autumn be far behind?

We planned the weekend carefully. It was the occasion for honoring mothers and we wanted to be sure the one at our house wouldn't be subjected to such back-breaking chores as twisting the dial on the oven or placing soiled items in the dishwasher.

We thought it would be a grand idea to get her out into the fresh, clean air. So we invited her to go fishing. As a bonus, we promised to bait her hook and to remove any fish she brought to the net.

Naturally, she was thrilled. She even agreed to share the rear seat of the car with Abe of Spoon River, our brilliant but sensitive Labrador Retriever, and promised not to interrupt the man talk except under extreme provocation. This girl is a good sport.

Actually, we were pleased to have her along. She is good company and surprisingly accomplished with a fly rod. Oh, she never catches anything but the fly almost always lands in the water. Once a friend praised her fly-casting form and the way she preened and postured for several days — well, you would have thought he had told her she would look great in a bikini.

We have decided to renew her option indefinitely because she is an expert and imaginative cook, she is handy at running errands, and she can communicate wth Abe of Spoon River. This dog is so intelligent he gives anybody with a limited vocabulary an inferiority complex. The distaff member of the household was the first to perceive this.

Suddenly she began spelling certain key words in the presence of our four-legged genius.

Naturally, we were amused. "You act like this dog is a precocious child! Pretty soon you'll be telling us he's won a scholarship to Cal Tech."

The lady lifted her nose imperiously. "You have to be careful what you say around this gifted fellow," she warned. "He is very bright but he is n-e-u-r-o-t-i-c."

Later it was noticed the genius was acting very much like a dog. He was scratching himself. Scratching himself in the presence of guests. He scratched with one hind foot, then the other. Seemed to enjoy it, too.

"This is embarrassing," said one of the males in the family. "Abe is behaving in a very bourgeoise manner. Next thing you know he'll be biting his nails and licking his plate. He must have picked up fleas somewhere."

Abe has a pedigree that goes back to the day when Labrador was an ice cap. By comparison, the Duke of Malborough is a peasant. Abe should have gone to Mayos for treatment but our errand girl took him to a vet.

"It isn't fleas," she said, confidently, "I told you he is n-e-u-r-o-t-i-c."

Sure enough. The vet looked him over and the diagnosis confirmed the lady's judgment. Abe was "emotionally disturbed." The vet prescribed a tranquilizer daily, a tranquilizer concealed in a ball of hamburger meat.

There was talk of sending Abe to a psychiatrist, but the idea was abandoned. Better to have a neurotic dog than sell the house. Besides there's little wrong with the genius that autumn won't cure.

Abe is a hunter and there is nothing worse than spring and summer. No quail or duck or pheasant to flush and retrieve. Just fishing. The males come out now and then wearing clothing that suggest fun and adventure, but they carry fishing rods instead of shotguns.

The fishermen permit Abe to accompany them, but it is a lost cause. Whoever heard of retrieving a bass? Or a trout? And it can be downright unpleasant. Once Abe sat on a small lure — a popping bug with a barbed hook — and when he got up the lure accompanied him.

Perhaps this is when he became n-e-u-r-o-t-i-c. The errand girl took him to the vet and the vet gave him an anaesthetic. The popping bug was gone when he awakened but Abe looked like he had been celebrating New Year's eve for a month. His eyes were red and sunken and he had the woebegone manner of an innocent betrayed by a cruel world.

Abe still goes along on special occasions — Mother's Day, National Smile Week and Cinco de Mayo — but he doesn't trust most fishermen, not even ones with impressive vocabularies. He dutifully returns the training dummy when it is flung into a lake or stream, and he pretends he doesn't understand when the lady says he is n-e-u-r-o-t-i-c.

The lady smiles when she spells the work, and often she rubs him behind the ears and permits him to lie on her feet. She's all right, even though she goes fishing. She's a good sport.

DUBLIN — It was too wet for golf and too cold for fishing, and thus we sought shelter and enlightenment in the library founded in 1702 by Narcissus Marsh, the Archbishop of Dublin.

In the study of Marsh Library we came across the Very Rev. V.G. Griffin, the dean of St. Patrick's Cathedral and successor to Jonathan Swift.

Swift had been installed as the dean of St. Patrick's in 1713 and held the office until his death in 1745. Yet, in the minds of some Americans, the author of "Gulliver's Travels" is still a very real presence.

The incumbent dean was chuckling about a letter he had received only two years ago addressed to Jonathan Swift, St. Patrick's Cathedral. The letter came from a gentleman in Texas who was writing a scientific paper related to agriculture and he sought Swift's permission to quote a passage from "Gulliver's Travels".

Naturally, Rev. Griffin decided the letter was a joke and tossed it into a wastebasket. But soon came another letter from the same source and this time the tone was more insistent. The scientist explained his publication date was approaching and imploring Swift to respond with all possible haste.

Then the Dean of St. Patrick's composed a reply which began: "I wish to advise that Jonathan Swift left here in 1745, destination unknown. We do not anticipate he will return in the forseeable future. However, knowing of the generosity of Swift, I feel sure he would not object if you wish to quote briefly from 'Gulliver's Travels'."

Such are the misconceptions one is apt to acquire of Ireland and the Irish. Perhaps you'll be surprised by the information that St. Patrick's Cathedral is of the Church of Ireland and the dean is an Episcopalian minister. The Roman Catholics do not have a cathedral in Dublin.

I had read of the ghost which supposedly inhabits the vicarage across the street from the cathedral and Marsh Library and, since the dean lives there, I asked him about it.

"I hope to meet the ghost in the vicarage one day," came the reply, "because I would like to interview him and sell an article to a magazine for a huge sum of money. Unfortunately, I've never had the opportunity."

A delightful man, the dean. And his cordial manner is typical of the people, high and low, one meets in going about Ireland. A few days previously we had stopped to ask directions at the Blue Diamond Pub in the tiny community of Letterfrack in Connemara and there we met a charming old fellow who urged us to stay and visit a spell.

"I'm a Dublin man," he explained, "but I once worked in America and I have a kindly feeling for Americans."

He had been a laborer for the Goodyear Rubber Co. in Akron, Ohio, and then he had returned to Ireland and, when his wife died five years ago, he settled in Connemara where there are numerous lakes and abundant numbers of trout and salmon.

He urged us to try a wet fly in the still waters of the Connemara version of the Holy Sea — a pretty lake which belongs to the Kylemore Abbey.

"See the nun in charge for permission to fish," he advised. "She drives a hard bargain — she'll charge you a pound for the day."

In truth, we have not killed many fish in Ireland. But the quest has been great fun and I hope to return another time — perhaps in summer when the rain is less frequent and the water is warmer and the only way to avoid catching trout is to stay at the hotel with the doors locked and curtains drawn.

I have been traveling in the pleasant company of Murray Olderman, a talented writer-artist out of San Francisco, and we've had a grand time despite our varying enthusiasms. Olderman is a golf nut and my game is fishing, and we've tried without success to convert each other.

But this is of no great consequence. We've seen a lot of Ireland in a brief time, we've been enriched by the kindly, hospitable people who have welcomed us everywhere, and the country has surprised us many times, always agreeably. When we passed through Belfast, the capital city of Ulster seemed perfectly serene.

I keep remembering the words of golf pro Fred Daley..."It would be very hard for a man to be lonely in

Ireland: and isn't that a nice thing to say about a country?''

SALISBURY, England — We had timed our arrival in the British Isles to coincide wth the summer solstice. Everybody is entitled to an aberration and I had agreed to humor my son in his ambition to visit Stonehenge, England's most celebrated prehistoric monument, on the occasion when the sun rises directly over the heel stone.

As it developed, we rose much earlier than the sun. Quite sensibly, the sun arrived at 9 a.m., boring through a thick morning fog. But then, we felt rather shaggy. Along with thousands of other pilgrims — a euphemism for hippies — we had reached the scene five hours earlier.

Stonehenge has been a source of awe and mystery for thousands of years. I wouldn't presume to explain it. Astronomer Gerald S. Hawkins has decided it was a calendar for determining eclipses of the sun and moon. Henry James termed it "lonely in history". It might have been an ancient religious temple or the site of pagan ceremonies.

Whatever its function, Stonehenge is endlessly fascinating and now the hippies have adopted it. On the morning of the summer solstice the area around Stonehenge was a hippie encampment. Hairy and barefooted, the boys and girls bundled in blankets or strolled about while a battalion of police watched for indications of mischief.

In other years vandals have disrupted the Druids'

solstice ceremonies and defaced the stones with paint. Now the police are about in substantial numbers and they have taken the precaution of ringing the monument with rolls of barbed wire. It's a bizarre scene, reminiscent of the barricades in Belfast but, happily, without violence and the gunfire.

Standing behind the barbed wire, the hippies were sullen but not mutinous. Two youngsters walked past, one playing a flute, the other a harmonica. They formed little circles, huddling against the early morning chill, and sang in sweet voices to the soft accompaniment of a guitar. One enterprising young man attempted to penetrate the barrier with wire clippers but the scheme aborted when he was seized by the gendarmes.

But solstice at Stonehenge isn't exclusively an attraction for hippies. Among the hairy types stood a young couple dressed in tuxedo and evening gown, the girl with her back uncovered and shivering in the cold. A chap who might have been a professor or an anthropologist came along in a tweed suit and weskit and stumbled over a girl sleeping in a bed roll. The girl didn't stir.

There were hundreds of dogs — every Englishman, it seems, goes about attached to one end of a leash with a poodle, a Labrador, a dachshund, a beagle, a boxer or a Jack Russell at the other. I first encountered a Jack Russell, a small friendly animal trained to chase foxes, in the bar at the Rose and Crown in nearby Harnham. This was a dog named Patch and he amused himself by trotting about the room with a cardboard coaster in his mouth. Evidently he doesn't care for bitters.

In any event, there were dogs of all descriptions at Stonehenge. Dogs, hippies, children, conservatively dressed townspeople and students, a few American tourists, lots of police with their helmets and blue uniforms, television cameramen with their beards and bright lights, and a group in flowing white robes who represent themselves as Druid priests.

The Druids are part of the legend of Stonehenge,

though scientists dispute their claims. The Druids believe the huge stones on the dramatic Salisbury plain are a heritage of their ancestry, but Stonehenge is probably 3,500 to 4,000 years old and that pre-dates the arrival of the Druids in England.

As the morning light became brighter, the Druids stood among the ancient stones and did whatever it is they do while TV crews recorded the ceremony and the hippies watched languidly behind the barbed wire barrier. Then the Druids formed a procession, walking in a single line in their robes and sandals, very solemn and important, and disappeared into a tunnel that leads to a parking area across the highway.

Thus ended the solstice at Stonehenge. Police began clearing the area, the hippies gathered their blankets, bed rolls and guitars, and straggled down the highway toward Amesbury, a distance of two and one-half miles. Others roared away on motorcycles or in small cars and a few gathered in the paved parking lot to make morning tea and prepare breakfast. The aroma of bacon and eggs frying in a skillet motivated the tourist to return in haste to his pad in Salisbury.

Later, the countryside would be free of traffic and quiet again, and the barbed wire would be removed and the police, red-eyed from lack of sleep, would climb into their buses and vans and disappear over the horizon of the brooding plain.

We didn't see the sun rise over the heel stone at Stonehenge, but we didn't feel cheated.

Do Bears Have a Taste for Eggnog?

We reluctantly parted company with my son the back-packer after tagging along for the first two hours in the Yosemite high country.

The boy and his pal, Ken, were setting off in the wilderness for the first time without adult supervision and a spirit of adventure possessed them as they headed up the trail at Tenaya Lake. They were eager for the freedom this trip symbolized, yet they graciously curbed their impatience.

The mother of my son the backpacker had dozens of reasons why we should walk with the boys instead of leaving them at the trailhead.

"A beautiful day for a hike," she explained, "and I just love the walk, and I need the exercise and..."

"It's all right, Mom," said the heir, otherwise known as John Patrick, "we'll be pleased to have you go with us as far as you like."

We stepped along at a brisk pace, even though the boys were toting a staggering amount of weight on their packboards. They had prepared for this expedition with meticulous care and I had watched with growing fascination as they brought their new gear into the house.

After a while I was persuaded they surely would require a couple of pack horses. Then, as the equipment piled higher and higher, I suspected they might have to rent a van. But, incredibly, they somehow stuffed all that food and baggage into two large packs.

The neighbors seemed a bit startled when a pair of teen-agers popped out of the house dressed in full packs and bedding rolls for a trail run.

"John," said the lady next door, "if you're not back in an hour I'll notify your next of kin."

The heir wasn't amused. Backpacking is serious business and his zeal was apparent when his mother required him to become familiar with a needle in the event he had to administer anti-venom on the trail. He blanched at first but soon he was quite cheerful about sticking himself.

"It doesn't hurt a bit," he assured me.

Once I found him practicing on a lemon in the kitchen. He was shooting the lemon with water and it had a strange, puffy appearance.

"Hey, Dad, how about a lemonade?" he proposed.

I knew my son had been giving a lot of thought to the

freeze-dried food he'd be eating on the trail when he proposed a feast at home the night before his departure. He had reason to believe his mother would grant any wish just then and he requested steak and his favorite cold soup, gazpacho. He was later observed hugging his mother and telling her the gazpacho was a triumph, the very best she has ever made.

The viands he is now having on the trail are less exotic. I'm not quite sure what the boys will be eating the next few days, but they are amply fortified with vanilla eggnog.

Between them, they have enough eggnog for 12 servings and, if you like eggnog, that sounds about right for a six-day hike. Eggnog, I was advised, is an egg substitute. The aroma of eggnog hung about the house like incense.

"I hope bears don't like eggnog." said my son. "As a matter of fact, I hope we don't meet any bears."

This is a boy with a practical turn of mind. Sometimes. He departed on his first backpacking trip with two knives, a propane lantern, a pedometer, poncho, bed roll with air mattress, a ground cover, a small tent — and one shirt. The shirt on his back.

I neglected to ask if there's a bar of soap in that huge pack, but he'll be presentable for social occasions. Checking the medicine cabinet on our return, I noted the absence of a can of spray deodorant.

We drove the boys to the ranger station at Tuolumne Meadows where they obtained a fire permit and filed a hike plan. They had worked on the plan with loving care and they presented it proudly to the ranger. He regarded them with respect.

"Since you boys are experienced hikers," he said, "I know I don't have to tell you to be careful with fires and to pack out your trash."

I know two boys who think that ranger is a helluva fellow.

We walked with the boys on the trail for some two

miles and it was reassuring to see them going along easily, despite the 50-pound burdens on their backs. It was a lovely day in the High Sierra and we stopped now and again to give the boys a rest and to listen to the wind in the trees.

"This looks like mountain lion country to me," said the mother of my son the backpacker. She wasn't nervous, I guess, but I wondered why she tried to light the filter end of a cigarette.

We parted when we came to a stream that required wading.

"I wish you could walk with us a while longer," said my son. He is 18 but he seems so terribly young. We shook hands and the mother kissed her boy and the backpackers set off rapidly, not looking back. We watched until the trail turned and they disappeared into the trees.

Then, for a long while, we walked in silence. The mother spoke first.

"When they get back," she said, "I'm going to serve both gazpacho and pumpkin pie for his first dinner."

As you might suspect, my son the backpacker is very fond of pumpkin pie.

Chapter 8

THE TWILIGHT YEARS

It's more than just an easy word for casual goodbye;
It's gayer than a greeting, and it's sadder than a sigh.

Don Blanding,
"Aloah Oe: It's Meaning."

I can't recall when I've felt so guilty. Another wing shooting season was beginning and I was trying to sneak a shotgun out of the house without alerting my ailing friend, Abe of Spoon River.

It would be easier to sneak the sunrise past a rooster.

Abe is recovering from a violent experience. While we fished and hiked in the High Sierra recently, Abe was the victim of a mugging. He was assaulted by a surly Old English sheep dog and he wears scars of that encounter; on his right hind leg there is the most awful wound I've ever seen on man or beast. And there are bruises on his throat the size of walnuts.

Clearly, his health is not such he is ready to retrieve fallen doves. He can move about without difficulty and his appetite is healthy. But the wound is still open and raw and we must guard against infection.

Thus I am compelled to leave him behind, and he

regards me as a Judas. No, that isn't quite accurate. His friendship is such he doesn't accuse me — he searches himself for an explanation. His chin ducks close to the floor, his tail is still.

We are very close after 10 years, and we don't require a lot of conversation. He reminds me of my son in one of his intractable moods. The young man listens with polite attention, but I can tell he is unconvinced.

There is nothing logical about a man leaving the house with gun in hand and closing the door on his dog. Those are the facts. In Abe's mind, you can't bend them into something else.

Retrieving, he knows, is his job. It is bred into him down through a long line of illustrious Labradors. He waits for the hunting season as a ballplayer waits for spring. On hunting days his manner changes.

For months he has been drowsing like a hibernating bear. Now he is alert and aware. His head is up, his body language is expressive. He doesn't walk, he struts. Hunting, his job, gives him a sense of importance, of fulfillment. Half the joy of going hunting is sharing the dog's excitement.

This is a pleasure we have shared since Abe first crawled into my arms as a four-month-old puppy.

Once Abe insinuated himself into my life, I knew I wouldn't be interested in another breed of dog. He's a fine retriever, considering the amount of work I'm able to give him, but that is the least of his charm. Abe is loyal, brave, gentle and kind.

He was a sleek, lively puppy when we began hunting together that first season in Arizona, and I almost lost him. In the excitement of the shooting I didn't notice right away Abe had disappeared. A bit frightened, I turned back and began searching for him.

I found him struggling in the swift current of an irrigation canal; he was clawing frantically at the concrete slopes, unable to gain footing. I flung myself to the ground, seized his front legs and pulled him to safety.

Then he came close, shook himself, and showered me with water from the canal. This is the ritual of Abe and all Labradors.

When I consider Abe's virtues, I think of something Gene Mauch once said of Alvin Dark: "He is the kind of guy we'd all like to be if we had time." My dog has become slower, heavier and grayer with the passing years, but his disposition is unchanged.

There is a sweetness about him which escaped the ornery critter who attacked him. I watch my wife tenderly ministering to his wound, Abe quivering but cooperating, the ideal patient, and I am filled with remorse because we left him behind to go fishing.

We reasoned he would suffer from the heat during our passage across the desert. Now we have the wisdom of hindsight and I wonder if he really will heal faster because my wife conceals vitamin E tablets in a ball of venison hamburger. The tidbit is his reward for being a good patient, and he loves being pampered.

Abe's nurse winces as she dresses the wound, but her voice croons and her face is alight when she feeds him the meatball. Two animal doctors have assured us he will mend swiftly, he'll be off the disabled list before the quail fly in October.

This is a thing to be devoutly wished. Going hunting and telling Abe he is being left behind for his own well being is a disagreeable business. My credibility is in tatters.

The Cat Has a Hero

We are waiting for Clovis, the confused tomcat, to develop a limp. Clovis is a cat who prefers the society of dogs, and he is devoted to our gentle Labrador Retriever, Abe of Spoon River. Abe is his hero; the cat models himself after the dog so closely we expect him to begin barking at any time.

Lately Abe has developed a limp. He was severely

wounded in a dogfight during the summer, but the limp stayed after he had healed. We tend to think of it as a sympathy limp, or a limp of convenience.

He begins carrying his right hind leg when he suspects neglect. There is an antenna in his old black head which enables him to know what others are thinking. He is never surprised when we leave the house and assign him to guard duty. But he's ingenious.

The limp serves him well. He looks so pathetic, hobbling about on three legs, the other dangling. His eyes petition for sympathy. Of course, we can't abandon a cripple. My wife hugs him tenderly I am tempted to carry the old fraud to the car.

But he reveals himself on the occasions when I go bird shooting. I remove a shotgun from the gun cabinet and Abe is squirming at my feet. No hint of a limp. His manner says he is still young and frisky; he's not old, just experienced.

He is a fine hunting dog because he is birdy. His nose fills with the delicious scent of quail and his tail transmits a message. When he is close to birds, the tail becomes very busy.

Hunting is pure joy to Abe. If I didn't restrain him, he'd hunt alone. My role is incidental.

I try to maintain order with a whistle. When he is excited Abe might ignore a spoken command but he responds to the whistle. The whistle speaks with authority.

When Abe seeks to please, he will work back and forth a few yards ahead of me, allowing the birds to flush within gun range. He pauses frequently to note my whereabouts and he will retrace his steps if he has strayed too far.

He is obliged to adjust to a hearing defect. I blow the whistle and I see him looking about as though trying to locate the sound. Then I make an arm signal, and he comes running.

At other times he is just plain obstinate. He'll run off and hunt with Jay, a fine Labrador who belongs to my friend, Bob Jordan. I don't much blame Abe. Surely it's more fun to hunt with another dog. I call him back and my tone is cranky. I raise hell.

Abe is unconcerned. That dog knows he can soften my anger with a look. How can you resist a dog who leans against you and offers a paw in friendship?

But that's nothing compared to the effect Abe has had on my wife. In the first place, she didn't really want a dog but chose not to oppose me in the interest of domestic peace. Dogs, she said, are dirty and smelly and, besides, they don't earn their keep.

Now I see her hugging Abe, loving him like a child.

"It's the strangest thing," she says, "but he smells good to me. I like his perfume."

Possibly this is also the attraction he holds for Clovis, the black and white tom who is marked like a panda. Clovis walks with Abe, sleeps at his feet, attempts (with mixed results) to share his food and becomes upset when Abe ignores him or goes hunting.

Soon I expect to find Clovis hiding under a shooting vest in the vehicle I use for hunting. But the tom has an exaggerated sense of his worth. Actually, he's a parasite.

When Abe is absent, Clovis walks in circles around my wife, yowling, complaining of being abandoned.

Yet he's just a pretty face. It's the female cat, Clotilde, who keeps us safe from our enemies. Clovis is a flower child.

Did You Ever See a Finer Head?

On other occasions I have told of how I first got acquainted with the dog who sleeps at my feet while I write and watches me with one eye open while I eat and dashes to the door when he hears the jingle of car keys.

Then he was a sleek and squirmy little fellow of four months. I innocently believed I had become the owner of a hunting dog of exceptional promise. But, in truth, Abe is the proprietor; he owns me.

Some time has passed since I took this Labrador Retriever home with me and named him Abe of Spoon River and I would say, on balance, he wears his years quite well.

His chin is flecked with gray whiskers and his hearing isn't what it used to be and, in certain seasons, he tends to become rather portly. He takes on weight at this time of year because wing shooting ends in February and that's one of the things we have in common.

Neither of us is greatly attracted to exercise without the motivation of hunting. We will cheerfully punish ourselves by scrambling through brush and chasing a covey of quail over rocky terrain that bristles with cactus. But we're not the kind of fellows who go jogging in a sweatsuit.

Just the other day my wife was saying that we'd better join the Weight Watchers or take up bicycle riding or running in place because summer is coming on and Abe doesn't stand heat very well. The day approaches when we'll be going to our little place in Montana for a holiday and there is a desert to cross en route. My wife reasons that if there's anything we don't need it's a large black Labrador scrambling into the front seat of our Jeep Wagoneer in order to benefit from the air conditioning.

So Abe has become a small consumer; he is on short rations. He will have a fine time in Montana; there is a rushing creek where he can refresh himself on hot days. There is lots of room to roam and fascinating scents to investigate. Every time I go to the creek with my fly rod I flush a covey of grouse.

These are some of the grace notes of human experience. But Abe isn't thinking of Montana. His stomach is a more immediate concern. The look in his eye speaks of an unfulfilled appetite.

Recently I was reading the information on Abe's registration certificate from the American Kennel Club.

His date of birth is June 27, 1963. He is the son of King Cole of Menomin and Odell's Nancy II. He is as black as coal and he has the most aristocratic head I've ever seen on a Labrador.

Now that he's eligible for Medicare, Abe is somewhat lumpy and shaggy but the head is as classic as ever. He is to Labradors what John Barrymore was to actors.

Abe reminds me of a fat woman with shapely legs. Other say, "look at that old dog." I say, "yes, isn't he handsome? Did you ever see a finer head on a dog?"

Abe is a friend I can enjoy because he is comfortable with silence. He comes into my study while I'm working and sits beside me. I stop and stroke him for a few seconds. That satisfies him; he just wants me to know of his interest. Then he leaves and sprawls on the tile entrance to the hallway. The tile is cool, it feels good against his belly.

It is my custom to build a fire in the evening and sit before the hearth with a book or magazine, puffing on a pipe and sometimes sipping from a snifter of brandy. Abe joins me there. He leans against me and moans when I stroke his head and scratch his ears. Often he offers his paw and I take it. This, I guess is his way of holding hands.

It would be an exaggeration to say I sleep better at night because Abe is there to watch over me. He's not guarding me, he's just sharing my company. Abe sleeps in the hall with his head just inside the bedroom. He's not allowed in the bedroom but he takes small liberties.

Abe wears a flea collar and a choke chain, and the choke chain is his bell. If he decides to go out during the night he stands in the hallway and shakes himself. The clatter of the chain awakens me. Sleepily, I arouse myself and turn him out.

Most of the year, in the seasons when he isn't finding and fetching birds, Abe is a non-contributing member of the family. The cats, Clovis and Clotilde, defend us against gophers and ground squirrels. Clotilde, ferocious

female predator, stands guard against rabbits.
Abe collects dust.

He comes in from the nearby fields matted with burrs.
He rolls in the dirt, his black coat turns red. He sheds
and leaves his hair in the kitchen. So my wife grumbles
about his sloppy ways. And adores him.

He does not seem so adorable when he chooses to go
out at the very time I have decided to go to bed. But I
wait for him to return, fighting sleep and feeling abused
because he is aging and arthritic and the chill night air
might harm him. Finally, I hear him scratching at the
door, scratching with mounting insistence if I have dozed
before the fire.

I bring him in and he rubs against me and touches my
hand with his nose. A good old dog, that Abe.

It was the occasion of Abe of Spoon River's 12th
birthday, and we made a proper fuss over the old chap,
granting him an extra portion of table scraps, and
hugging his neck, and letting him know he is greatly
appreciated.

My wife was rubbing his stomach while complaining
that this dog is outrageously pampered and he responded
with a Labrador Retriever's version of a grin.

The only time Abe shows his teeth is when he rolls on
his back with his four black paws in the air. Then his two
fangs are exposed and he looks fierce at one end and

sociable at the other. The thumping tail runs like a meter in a taxi and cancels the threat of the fangs.

"The time approaches," reflected my wife, "when we will communicate with him mostly through our hands."

Which is to say his eyesight is somewhat diminished; his hearing would be improved by an ear trumpet, and his step is considerably slower. Mostly, he sleeps. Wherever I move about the house I can hear the sound of his breathing.

When I address the typewriter in my spelling room, he snoozes beneath the desk. When I'm in the shower he makes his bed just outside the bathroom door. Sometimes he twitches and something in his dream stirs him to bark; other times he yelps in a small voice.

I imagine he is dreaming of late October and quail in flight. It should be a fine year for wing shooting. One of the blessings of spring rain is a bountiful hatch of quail.

On a recent morning I stopped the Jeep on a little used road in the north county and watched two quail hen in the company of 18 chicks. The chicks were about the size of a man's thumb, and they'll soon learn to fly into heavy brush when approached by two and four-legged predators.

As the quail marched across the road, I noticed that Abe had become short of breath. Then, suddenly, he was alert, his ears were up, he had the look of a young dog again. A hunting dog is not unlike a ballplayer; he never tires of batting practice.

I find it pleasing that both Abe and his breeder, Jay Odell, are enjoying good health and long life. By human standards Abe is 84 or thereabouts. Jay Odell will be 89 in November and younger men hurrry to match his pace when he takes long walks on the beach in La Jolla.

Jay expects to live 100 years because his dogs keep him young, and he is faithful to his herbs and elixirs. He begins each day with a dollop of scotch whiskey and ends it in the same fashion. He smokes an old pipe with a bent stem, competes aggressively at cribbage, wears a funny shapeless Irish hat, sleeps 10 hours each night, and turns down his hearing aid when the conversation bores him.

His bachelor son, Dave, a retired Air Force colonel, keeps him company when he isn't running off to field trials in Wyoming or watching the dogs work bobwhite quail on a plantation in South Carolina.

"Everybody knows my father is a character," says Dave, "and the longer he lives, the more of a character he becomes."

Odell is a crusty Scots Presbyterian who holds strong views about politics, religion, baseball, George Halas and free enterprise.

He is sentimental and generous and full of laughter. And hope.

Right now he is working on plans for the small home he intends to build on his farm in Illinois. His dogs are there in the care of a trainer and Jay will go to Crystal Lake during the wing shooting season to watch them work. The house will have a captain's walk to provide Jay with a vantage point; it will be an old bird hunter's version of an observation tower.

I can visualize him on the captain's walk: his hat at a rakish angle, four whistles hanging at stomach level, pipe and Odell aglow. Which countermands Brendan Gill's dictum that no good deed goes unpunished.

Odell is guilty of many good deeds, not the least being my companionship with Abe of Spoon River. I am greatly pleasured by the sight of my old dog rolling and romping on our new lawn, and I have to work at being cranky even when he leaps into a mountain lake where I am attempting to seduce a bass by twitching a top water plug.

A Labrador goes to water as surely as a drunk turns into a saloon. Abe regards me with astonishment and an attitude of injury when I reluctantly summon him from the lake and make him a prisoner of the Jeep.

I seek to explain that Labradors and bass are not a sporting pair, but he sits there and stares accusingly. Nevertheless, we are the best of friends after 12 splendid years in grassy and woody places. No fish, whatever its size, will ever come between us.

One of the reasons I'm so fond of my gentle Labrador Retriever, Abe of Spoon River, is that he seems to know writing is a lonely job.

When I seat myself before the typewriter in the cluttered study I call my spelling room, Abe comes quickly to offer an expression of support.

Softly I stroke his old black head and he leans against me.

I think he is saying, "It's you and me, boss. You can take as much time as you need. I'll wait."

Then he goes to a corner of the room and sprawls on the green shag rug. He is motionless except when his legs twitch in sleep.

My spelling room seems an agreeable place to Abe. It is here, on certain days, the fun begins. When I retrieve a shotgun from the gun cabinet, Abe's feet become active. He can no sooner be still than a drummer boy playing Dixie.

Dr. Arnold Mandell, the psychiatrist, has decided he can recognize the personalitites of pro football players by inspecting their dressing quarters. Offensive linemen tend to be neat and orderly. Defensive specialists leave their effects in disarray.

I don't know what Arnie would learn about my personality if he visited my study, but there are numerous clues. The occupant smokes a lot, there are many books on the shelves, and evidence of a man who finds pleasure in field and stream.

The decorative touches include a water color of Abe, with his old gray chin; mounted wood duck, faded decoys which have been subject to all the vagaries of weather, a hand-carved Canadian honker and an owl and a terrapin shaped from pine cones. And a cheerful water color print of the Mallard Hole at Venice Island, the best of places.

There's a gun cabinet loaded with rifles and shotguns, and three large ash trays abrim with pipes.

Arnie Mandell would probably decide the man who works here is straining to escape from his own tobacco fumes. But some work gets done. There's a typewriter, a desk, a large dictionary on a stand and even a filing cabinet.

Not to mention a dog whistle hung around the neck of a golf club. That whistle has meaning to Abe. When I retrieve the whistle, Abe opens one eye and shows interest. When I open the door to the gun cabinet and remove my favorite .20 guage, he scrambles to his feet.

There are two Abes. At home, he's a loving friend. In the field, he's a hunter who carries himself proudly like a grand prix jumping horse. The same dog who craves affection at home becomes aloof when we are pursuing quail.

When we pause to rest, I reach out to him and he seems irritated. He is impatient with such nonsense.

Yet this dog is so affectionate when I am dressing that lacing up my boots becomes a problem. As soon as I am seated and begin with the boots, Abe joins me. He bumps my hand with his nose, and the boot laces slip from my fingers.

I don't particularly like this chore, anyway. Usually the

hour is early, the house dimly lit, I am cheated of sleep. I need coffee, not a loving Labrador.

Man must seem awfully slow to a hunting dog. I hurry into my clothing and gulp down coffee so hot it burns my mouth. Abe goes to the hallway and waits at the door. He doesn't complain exactly. He sighs. Long, deep sighs. That's a comment.

I placate him by installing him in the Jeep while I gather the remainder of my hunting effects. The old chap is not spry as he used to be, and his flight to the tailgate of the Jeep can be exciting.

But we've worked it out. I've taught him to take a long run — indeed, I run with him — and he easily lands on the tailgate. Except, of course, when he's cold and a bit stiff. Then I give him a boost.

My friends say he is aging gracefully. Last hunting season he was overweight, he sometimes carried a hind leg badly torn in a dogfight, and he tired quickly. Now he is trim and athletic, as enthusiastic as a pup.

Some dogs, like some people, retain youthful appearance. The only clue of Abe's senior status is the gray hair on the underside of his chin. I sometimes wonder if he sneaks a few touches of black shoe polish. I would term him handsome.

And sensitive. My wife reports that he sulked a lot when I disappeared for a week because of a football game in New Orleans. If Abe thought about football, he would wonder why men bother to agitate a bag of wind.

When I returned, he tried to climb into the car with me as I opened the door. But it was rather crowded, with the steering wheel and all. Then we hugged each other for quite a spell.

Abe isn't the sort to mask his feelings. He was awfully glad to see me and he pressed against me and made peculiar sounds in his throat. I wouldn't want a talking dog — one hears too many voices already — but I appreciated the warmth of his welcome.

It's been said that a dog is man's best friend because

he's too smart to bite the hand that feeds him. But I can think of better reasons.

Abe Knows His Subject

We have been friends for almost 12 years, and I would say the relationship has been warm and pleasant. Seldom has an angry word passed between us.

I am sometimes troubled, however, that my shrewd black Labrador Retriever, Abe of Spoon River, seems to know more about people than I know about dogs.

It's probably unfair to say Abe has an advantage because he has nothing much to do but study me. I'll say it anyway because I don't like to admit, even to myself, that the dog is smarter than his master.

Call it ESP, or whatever, but Abe somehow has slipped himself into my subconscious. He knows what I'm going to do even before I've worked it out.

I'll get up in the morning with a half-formed idea about going somewhere other than to the office and Abe will take a lively interest in my activities. His breathing quickens, his tail becomes busy, his feet are restless.

I rub his ears and stroke his black blouse and urge him to compose himself.

"Sorry, Abe, but you're deluding yourself. Nothing interesting is going to happen today. You might as well forget it."

But Abe is unsurprised a while later when I decide the day is too nice to waste and we go to a nearby lake for some exercise with the training dummy. He sits by the door, head erect and proud, while I fetch the car keys. I imagine I can hear him chuckling in his old gray beard as he springs to the tailgate of the Jeep.

I think it is accurate to say our friendship is rooted in mutual respect. He credits me with a fair amount of intelligence; he has learned I am sensitive to his needs.

When he needs attention, he is much too well man-

nered to raise his voice. When he has an urge to leave
the house he just takes a station near the door and waits.
I can't see him when I am watching the flames cast
shadows in the fireplace, but he knows I am listening for
his steps. I can feel his presence.

Yet there is much I don't understand about this
remarkable dog. He is as eccentric as a poet.

He is bred for swimming in icy water, but why does he
cower at the door, demanding admission, when he is
splattered by a light rain?

Why does he sleep in the doorway of whatever room I
am occupying, making it necessary for me to step over or
around him? This can be tricky when one is carrying a
ladder or even a typewriter.

How does he know when fish is the featured item on
the evening menu? If the entree is meat, Abe springs
alertly to my side as soon as I push back my chair. If it's
fish, he remains flattened like a frog in the corner of the
room, snoring softly.

Why does he awaken me each morning at precisely
seven o'clock? Is there a timepiece in his head?

Why does he walk on my toes when I am barefoot?

How does he know I will soon be turning into the
driveway when I am still five minutes away and he can't
hear the sound of the car?

What can he hear? He affects deafness when scolded
for rubbing himself against the walls in the long hallway.
But he can hear a shotgun open, he is alert to the click of
the door of the gun cabinet, the muted tinkle of a car key
brings him running.

But, no matter. Mystery lends spice to our friendship.
Abe never asks me to explain myself; why should I probe
in his chest of secrets?

He is not only tolerant of his human companions, he
even indulges the whimsical behavior of our two cats,
Clovis and Clotilde. Clovis, the gelded tom, will press
himself against Abe for warmth while he sleeps on a chill
day. Abe shows no annoyance. Clotilde, the killer fe-

male, is a mischievous sort who sometimes leaps on Abe's back when he is dreaming of quail in flight. He grunts, shifts positions, and resumes his dream.

Great is the dignity of my friend Abe. If he were human, surely he would be a justice of the highest court. He has a sense of the fitness of things.

He would never enter a door without an invitation, leave a car without a signal, or eat until the dinner bell rings. He idea of demi-tasse is seeking the company of his mistress before the fire after the evening meal.

It's a nightly ritual, pleasant to behold.

The lady hugs his neck and speaks sweetly to him and the old chap holds a paw aloft, groans and presses closer. This, I would say, is pure contentment — and no mind that he sometimes tracks mud into the house, sheds black hair, and rubs black marks on the walls.

We don't ask perfection of each other; friendship freely given is just fine.

The red-tailed hawk who snatched a mouse from Clovis while he held it lovingly in his white paws wasn't tuned into the spirit of Christmas.

Neither was the shaggy gray coyote who came boldly into the floodlights which illuminate the piece of ground which houses all creatures great and small of Clan Murphy. The coyote had picked up the scent of our resident rabbit, Peter, who makes his bed beneath a Rosemary bush. Fortunately, the rabbit was off singing Christmas carols or doing whatever rabbits do in this season.

This year it feels more like the Christmas of Currier and Ives, the Christmas of Irving Berlin's song, the one that made us a bit misty-eyed when we were in distant places during World War II.

The December nights have bite in the north county, with the overnight temperature readings below 30 on occasion. There's been frost on the roof and one morning the water in the birds' drinking fountain was solid ice.

This was of concern because it's a community drinking fountain. The bluebirds flutter from the apricot tree to sip in their dainty fashion, and the sparrow hawk is an occasional caller. The watering hole also is favored by Abe of Spoon River, an old dog who becomes bouncy and frisky on chill mornings, and the cats, Clovis and Clotilde.

We come to this Christmas in a mellow mood. After 12 years on earth Abe is slower at finding and retrieving a bird, but he finds it. And he is great with joy.

The fellow who does the shooting walks a bit unsteadily at times because he got up one morning in July and found the house spinning about him; as he suspected, the problem was an inner ear infection. But no matter. He's getting about and finding much pleasure in life and every so often, to his astonishment and Abe's delight, a bird goes into the bag.

The one who carries the gun has changed only to the extent he tires more easily, and the one who fetches the birds needs a hearing aid. It takes a whistle to get Abe's attention and ear plugs to share his company.

As he becomes longer in the tooth, Abe's snoring is just a couple of decibels below a chain saw. Even now, as I write this, he is tucked at my feet beneath the desk.

The sound doesn't disturb, it pleases. Sometimes I

awaken during the night and I hear that old dog breathing deeply, and I am reassured. I don't even complain when he rouses me from beneath a snug goose down comforter, shaking his choke chain in my ear to announce it's time for his morning constitutional.

I delight in watching him as he jogs down the dirt road which leads to a neighbor's ranch, his tail switching, his nose investigating every fascinating scent along the way.

I have no idea if Abe and the coyote are acquainted, but it wouldn't be surprising. Abe is a tolerant sort; he would have no bias about coyotes. He's even tolerant of cats who leap playfully at his tail and groom his gray beard.

As you may suspect, this dog pleases me. His only serious fault is that he often sleeps in doorways or in the hall and he has tripped more people than the Chargers' special teams. Further, he has the regrettable habit of raising his head just as one is stepping over him.

After accidentally booting him in the jaw several times, I gave this problem intense thought and arrived at a solution. The lesson I learned is to let sleeping dogs lie. Which is to say you step over the end that wags and avoid the end which eats and snores.

Abe is the only member of the family who seems unimpressed by our Christmas tree. The cats are enchanted with the lights and bright ornaments, and my wife generously concedes I couldn't have found a more comely tree.

It doesn't matter so much now that we had a terrible time persuading the tree to stand as it should, or that it pitched over a few times and just missed shattering my favorite painting.

Our home seems especially attractive on this Christmas day, it imparts a feeling of warmth. The tree is splendid, the hearth glows with the flames of burning oak, my wife has fashioned lovely pine wreaths for the entry from the lower limbs of the Christmas tree, a long row of candles casts a soft light from the window boxes,

Christmas cards bring cheery greetings from friends, and, of course, there's a sprig of mistletoe.

Quite a bit of kissing and smiling and hugging is going on around here, and that's not a bad custom on Christmas day.

Or any other day.

'The House Feels Cozy and Right'

One comes blinking into the California sunlight after an experience approaching total immersion in the Innsbruck Winter Games, and it is comforting to find the land has been blessed by rain and the wild creatures have raised their voices in celebration.

We are groggy with jet lag after flying the polar route from London — passing through eight time zones and slipping into the United States just north of Great Falls, Montana — but my wife is enchanted by the sounds of home.

A pair of horned owls is hooting a mysterious message, and it pleases my wife to believe they are calling a greeting. The rabbit she knows as Peter hops from the Rosemary hedge and regards us shyly. A chorus of bullfrogs at a nearby farm's pond croaks in the stillness of night; their music is as sweet as an Alpen horn.

The look of fatigue leaves my wife.

"Now," she says, "it feels like home."

She'd rather be welcomed by a pair of hoot owls than the mayor and a symphony orchestra. But the house lacks warmth to me because I am awaiting the arrival of an old black dog.

Every time I saw a dog in Innsbruck or Seefeld or wherever we traveled, I had an itch for the company of Abe of Spoon River. And that was pretty often because Europeans are daft about dogs.

I watched women carrying poodles into a tea room at Harrads in London, and dogs were as welcome as other tourists in the finest restaurants of Innsbruck. At Seefeld, the mountain resort above Innsbruck, there were long-haired dachshunds who sank to stomach level in the fresh snow and wore fashionable white chin whiskers.

That put me in mind of Abe, whose chin is frosty with age, not with snow. He is deaf as a post. I am advised he can't reasonably anticipate more than one more season of wing shooting; he is eligible for Medicare, Social Security and senior citizens' rates at ball games. But I resist the idea of signing an understudy.

There have been a lot of dogs in my life — German shepherds, collies, mongrels, poodles, just about everything but a Great Dane or a St. Bernard. But Abe is special.

During the night following our arrival, while I was woozy from flying a third of the way around the world, I awakened at dawn and heard the high soprano voices of our neighborhood coyotes. Nice.

I love to hear coyotes and I try, unsuccessfully, to fight off sleep so their music will not be lost. When I was a small boy growing up in Oklahoma, I listened for rain on the roof; the rain was my sedative.

Now I hear the coyotes and I am pleased. I awaken from a deep sleep, remembering an odd dream; I have been interviewing Arnold Palmer. Why not Dorothy Hamill?

The coyotes bring me back to reality and I listen for the sound of Abe's breathing. The house is silent. It seems cold without Abe. Then I remember: Abe is in the care of two beloved friends, Bob and Marian Jordan.

The Jordans generously take Abe into their home when we go to distant places. He knows he is welcome there; he is received as an honored guest both by the Jordans and their playful Labrador, Jay. Abe and Jay are cousins, they have a fine rapport. They are even good humored about competing for space before the fireplace.

We had a joyous reunion when Bob and Marian delivered Abe to our embrace. He gets so much love from the Jordans I'm doubtful he shared our excitement.

But he greeted us enthusiastically, and now the house feels cozy and right. His presence is cheering.

The small pleasures are best. When we were in Innsbruck it was grand to awaken each morning, open the drapes, and gaze at the scenic Tyrolean Alps. The nights were agreeable, too. What better way to drift off to sleep than by listening to happy Austrian youngsters yodeling on the streets below?

Now I am truly at ease in my study when Abe comes to my side, gives my left arm a nudge, and offers his head for caress. Satisfied, he then sprawls in the doorway. He wants me to know of his presence; he is rooting for me, I am not alone, he has faith in me.

This can be reassuring to a man blinking at an empty page, a man who bites on the stem of his pipe because he craves inspiration. Abe is aware. As Bob Jordan has taught me, a Labrador, the right Labrador, knows your most secret thoughts. He knows if you are anxious, he knows if you are serene. It goes beyond vibrations, good and bad. He has given you much study and thought. The dog knows the man better than man knows the dog.

That being true, and I have no reason to doubt it, Abe is secure in the knowledge I am pleased to have his company again. He's been missed.

One definition of a gentleman is a man who can disagree without being disagreeable. It also serves to describe my friend Abe of Spoon River, a most elderly

Labrador Retriever who disputes the judgment of his personal physician but does it with style and diplomacy.

Abe acknowledged his 13th birthday in late June and it wasn't long thereafter we learned he was in fragile health. During the course of a routine examination, it was determined he had a diseased heart.

The vet, who is very fond of Abe, showed me the reading of the electrocardiogram and explained the significance.

He suggested I'd better not make any long term plans for Abe. And he recommended that I retire him as a hunting companion.

"The old fellow can't handle much stress," he warned, "take him hunting and you might lose him."

Abe and I went home and thought it over, and decided to disagree with the vet. Actually, Abe decided. I got my things together for an afternoon of wing shooting and Abe stalked me from the gun cabinet to the car. He was dancing about with his head proud and erect — a look I have come to know so well through the years — and his eyes were soft and imploring.

I melted. I boosted my friend into the car and he dissolved into a bundle of contentment. We had a fine day; the doves were flying, Abe made a few retrieves and came home with feathers on his chin. That night he slept very soundly, curled at my feet.

When I had a chance, I made a full confession to the vet. Better Abe should have some pleasure in his remaining time, I reasoned, than live longer and perish of boredom.

The vet smiled. "Of course you're right," he said, gently. "He's bred for hunting, it would be a pity to deprive him of the thing he most enjoys. But it is important that you understand the risk."

So, with luck, we will have another season together; I won't be sneaking out of the house to avoid Abe's accusing eyes, I won't leave my friend at the door, feeling cheated.

It's reassuring, too, that he has the best of care and is responding to treatment. Twice each day his nurse, also a loving and good-humored housewife, doses him with digitalis, a medicine made from the leaves of purple foxglove.

This is accomplished with a medicine dropper, and Abe is a most cooperative patient. Why not? The nurse not only gives him a squirt of digitalis but hugs his neck.

Abe is feeling pretty frisky for an elderly party with a tricky heart. The latest EKG shows that his heartbeat is normal again and he looks grand because he's been dieting and has lost 10 pounds.

The vet determines his weight by cradling Abe in his arms and standing on the scales. Abe gains weight only when the vet eats pasta at his evening meal.

On a recent evening Abe came loping into the yard, a dim figure in the twilight, and his nurse greeted him in the most flattering way.

"Abe," she said, "I didn't recognize you. You are so thin I thought you were a young dog."

Maybe it was only my imagination, but I'd swear Abe blushed and scuffed a toe in the lawn.

If this is Abe's last season, it should be one of our best. The biologists of Ducks Unlimited promise great flights of wildfowl when the Canadian weather tells them it's time to migrate, and the backcountry is acrawl with quail.

We've been here and there in search of a large buckskin with a fancy hatrack and the birds explode from business and tease us with their presence. Chickens, my friend Willie Tellam calls 'em.

"Look at the chickens," he exults when a covey of quail takes flight. We'll be back later to attend to the chickens.

Presently we are involved with what might be described as hunting without malice aforethought. Really, the idea is to escape from typewriters and other forms of work and to prolong the season until the last day. This is best accomplished by waiting for a trophy buck. Our system wouldn't please the Friends of Animals, but it's an effective form of conservation. In the past three years I have used one rifle cartridge.

This doesn't make points with my son, who is keen about venison. But it enables us to avoid work throughout the season, and we experience much pleasure.

On a recent afternoon we admired many deer, we watched with delight and laughter as a coon scrambled up a tree, and we stared at a bobcat who, in turn, regarded us in his chilly fashion. That gray and white cat was beautiful in his way but he had a demeanor that discouraged fraternizing. His body language was decidedly hostile.

The cat amused Tellam. "Do you think it would be a good idea," he asked, "to say 'here, kitty, kitty' and pick him up?"

We left the nice kitty to his own devices, and enjoyed a lovely afternoon that had the texture of high mountains. The backcountry is extraordinarily lush and green in this season, its beauty floods the senses. In the time that remains, Abe will have a chance to enjoy it.

He is special in many ways, but I wouldn't want to claim that Abe of Spoon River is the only Labrador Retriever who received attention from both a physician and a private nurse.

Abe's health has been a concern since last September when a routine medical examination revealed he is afflicted with heart disease. It was then his physician sketched a program which would keep Abe together through another season of bird hunting, the activity that brings joy to his sere years.

A good plan, evidently; it looks as though Abe is going to make it with the help of digitalis, dilantin and lots of loving care. Twice each day his nurse squirts digitalis down his throat with a medicine dropper, then presents him with a cheese ball which conceals a dilantin tablet.

Which explains a plastic container in the refrigerator with an odd label: "Abe's Cheese Balls." Abe regards the cheese balls as a reward for being such a cooperative patient; he doesn't even suspect they are part of the treatment.

Of course, he isn't the dog he used to be. His most recent birthday, June 27, was his 13th, the human equivalent of 91 years or thereabouts. I suppose it's not so remarkable that Abe still demands hunting privileges, though he has to be indulged in matters of no consequence.

George Halas, owner of the Chicago Bears, is 82 and he still rides a bicycle every day unless ice and snow interfere. I have to boost Abe to the tailgate of the Jeep Wagoneer, it is sometimes necessary to help him through a barbed wire fence, and he'll find a shady place and rest when he tires.

My longtime friend and hunting companion, Bob Jordan, has counseled that I should devote this hunting season to Abe because it surely will be his last and this I have done. When Abe signals he wants a break, I humor him gladly.

But he is bred for hunting, he is impatient with the limitations of his age. I saw this very clearly on a recent morning while in pursuit of quail. It was a cool, pleasant day, just right for an old dog, but Abe wanted to rest. I waited with him. He put his chin in the dirt and took a nap.

He must have resented the weariness that possessed him. After a few minutes the sound of a shotgun was heard. Bill Tellam was adding to his bag of birds. Abe's head came up, alert. His tail began swishing along the ground. The report of the gun excited him. He got to his feet, he looked at me expectantly.

It was a fine day for Abe. He picked up a number of birds, most of which belonged to Bill Tellam and his son, John. That's one reason to have a good dog. I don't harm much wild life, I have a deserved reputation as a conservationist, but I get lots of birds.

I need Abe because I have a wife who draws the line at retrieving ducks. She'll make cheese balls for the dog, but she won't respond to my whistle or hand signals. I guess that's why I'm so impressed by Eileen Tellam. She's a triple threat — wife, school marm, and retriever.

The Tellams are in the cattle business, thus they have dogs who will nip the legs of a steer instead of dogs who will swim after ducks. When Bill dropped several ducks of a flight rising from a lake near their home at Witch Creek, he had fresh reason to appreciate Eileen.

It was a warm day but the icy water discouraged skinny dipping. Nevertheless, Eileen swam to the middle of the lake, picked up the birds and returned them without a whimper.

"A great girl," said Bill, "though she got a little tired on the last retrieve."

Since Eileen isn't always available for such activity, Bill lately has been experimenting with a small, feisty dog named Henry. Henry is bred for putting cattle over a fence, he's an Australian collie, but he has developed a lively interest in quail.

Henry can't smell the birds, but he can see them. He's a wonder at flushing a quail from a blackberry thicket. In his fashion, he's also a retriever. When a bird dropped in a creek bed Henry found it and pinned it with one of his paws until Bill arrived.

The dog delights Bill. But now that Henry has discovered the charm of hunting, Bill fears he has been corrupted.

Bill reasons, "When we're rounding up cattle and Henry goes off chasing quail, I'll have myself to blame."

Goodbye, Old Friend

The instant I answered the phone I sensed that something was dreadfully wrong.

"Have you finished writing?" asked my wife. She was striving for a casual tone.

"No, I'll be a while. Why do you ask?" I could hear alarm bells ringing.

"The neighbors have just brought word a dog was hit by a car down the street. I'm afraid it's Abe. I can't bear the thought of seeing him. The neighbors are with him, I've called Frank Goldsmith, he's coming right away."

I put the phone back in its cradle and tried to focus on the half-finished piece in my typewriter. The words, poor words, formed through a mist. I knew my beloved Labrador Retriever, Abe of Spoon River, was dead.

Later I would learn that a kindly neighbor woman had covered him with a blanket and lay beside him to give him the warmth and comfort of her body.

"I wanted him to know he wasn't alone," she said.

But life had left Abe's old body. Frank Goldsmith, a veterinarian who loves and ministers to animals in Rancho Bernardo, had closed his office and hurried to Abe's side when the summons came.

He listened for a heartbeat and searched for a pulse.

"He's gone," said the vet. His voice was a whisper.

It was Goldsmith's medicine and care that prolonged Abe's useful, happy life for the past year. Abe couldn't beat the heart disease that drained him, but the medicine gave him an extra season of fun and games. It was borrowed time, and we cherished it.

The vet is a sensitive man. After attending to Abe, he sought to console my wife.

"The blow killed him instantly," he said, "he knew no pain, he never cried or whimpered."

Then he pressed something into my wife's hand and squeezed her arm. When my wife opened her hand she found Goldsmith had brought her Abe's shiny choke chain.

Now the chain is draped around a golf club in my study along with the whistle he heard so often before deafness blotted out the sound in his last year. These are symbols of the pleasure we knew during a friendship of 13 years. It had been such a glorious time, and now there was only pain.

Pain, but no bitterness. The woman who had the bad luck of hitting Abe with her car came to our door in tears to express her sorrow. She had no chance to spare him. A black dog sauntering along an unlighted street, a bump in the night, and Abe was dead.

I won't try to tell you how much I miss that dog. But I suppose it's all right to say I listen for his toenails scratching the door, I want to hear him snoring beside my bed, I am puzzled when he doesn't awaken me before the rooster stirs, I wait for him to nudge my arm when I am busy at my desk.

Abe is everywhere in the house, but I can't find him.

"The house seems empty without Abe," says my wife, who loved him equally.

Our senses are flooded with memories, everywhere there are reminders of his presence. Walls and rugs are stained with dirt where he rubbed and rolled, there's a half consumed can of meat in the refrigerator; this morning I washed and stored the pan that was his serving dish. It always delighted me to hear his choke chain clanking against his pan.

Our last three days with Abe were among our best.

The first day, acting on impulse, we hoisted Abe into the Jeep Wagoneer and drove to a ranch near Julian where we gathered kindling and strolled in the sweet sunshine.

Abe investigated the bushes for scent of quail and, after a time, he wandered off with my wife while I followed a trail where a golden eagle sometimes resides. When we were reunited, Abe came to me running.

"He's been searching for you," said my wife. "He didn't see you leave. He was awfully worried."

Then we came upon a pretty stream. I heard a splash. Abe had jumped into the brook, he was wet up to his chin, his wagging tail signaled his delight.

On the following days we took long walks on the farm near our home, Abe springing to his feet as soon as I showed him my hickory walking stick. He was indifferent when meadowlarks took flight in a weedy pasture, but expressed interest in mourning doves flapping overhead. Abe knew we sometimes eat doves, but have no interest in meadowlarks.

He walked along slowly, his breathing was labored and noisy. I felt concern. Then something would engage his interest, he'd break into a trot, and I was reassured. Every hour, every moment, was becoming precious.

"I fear he won't be with us much longer," I told my wife. When we returned to the house I opened the door for Abe and he thanked me by nudging my hand with his nose.

The last day began like all the others. I reached out and felt Abe beside the bed as I awakened, I stroked his old head tenderly as I left for the office. I never saw him again.

Epilogue

Abe sleeps now in a pretty place near a waterfall where one can hear quail calling and where deer browse when the light is soft at the beginning and end of day. It pleases me to think of my old friend resting while a bird with a topknot whistles in his ear.

I still look about for Abe and listen for the sound of him at the door, impatiently demanding entrance. But the pain is gone and the void has been filled to an extent by a shiny, squirmy puppy. We choose to call him Jacob of Green Valley.

He comes to us from the Illinois kennel of Jay G. Odell, who bred Abe. When Jay learned of Abe's death, he sent a brief note. "Can't write more — paper too damned wet," he apologized.

But now he has sent us a spendid black male Labrador Retriever puppy and I have high hopes for Jake. All I want of him is that he fetch birds, columns and friends, as did Abe. My wife and I promise to love him in return.

--Jack Murphy